Life Abroad @ Handong

To: Bob & Jan —

Thank you for your ENCOURAGEMENT AND PRAYERS!

GRACE & PEACE,

Gordon

1 THESS. 5:21

Life Abroad @ Handong

*Some lessons still being learned
by a would-be teacher*

Cordell Patrick Schulten

After ten years practicing law and another fifteen teaching at universities in Saint Louis, Missouri, I was invited to teach American law at Handong Global University in Pohang, Korea. In these pages, I recount some experiences and lessons learned during my life abroad at Handong.

Contents

Preface 8

Calling

    1. Come and See 12

Waypoints

    2. Handong International Law School 18

    3. A Few More Steps along the Way 47

First Year

    4. Reminders along the Journey 54

    5. "Hop-along" -- My New Korean Name 69

    6. Six Degrees of Separation or is it Just Two?. 96

    7. An Occasion to Teach 115

    8. To Question or Not to Question? 133

Second Year

    9. A Walking-Paced Life 144

    10. First Day's Daunting. 152

    11. A Teacher's Dilemma 159

12. A Letter of Decision 170

13. Hahoe Village -- The Williamsburg of Korea. 180

Third Year

14. An Emerging Korean Call 192

15. Playing the Fool . . . and Teaching, too 217

16. Campaign for a Balanced Life 228

17. "I perceive that you are very religious" 234

Reflection

18. You don't need a Map, when you have a Guide. . . 242

Acknowledgements

Paul wrote to the believers he had lived among and taught in Thessalonica, "For what is our hope or joy or crown of boasting before our Lord Jesus at his coming? Is it not you? For you are our glory and joy." (1 Thessalonians 2:19-20) After my years living, teaching, and learning abroad at Handong, I have a come to understand the feelings within the heart of Paul when he wrote those words.

I offer continuing thanks to God for the love and grace shown to me by the ones who I am now privileged and blessed to call my glory and joy. I could not have thrived, let alone survived, at Handong without the gracious help and daily assistance from my faithful teaching assistants: Younghoon Mok, Juyoun Han, YeEun Han, Jiyun Moon, Areum Ryo, Seo Kyong Go, Dayeon Won, Hannah Lee, Sangil Moon and Kwang Hyun Park. Three students were and continue to be my special support and research assistants: Haeun Jang, Yating Du, and Ellena Walker. My extra special recognition and undying gratitude extends to Boyeon Han and Damiya Park for their insightful and invaluable editorial assistance. It is my heart's true joy to see you becoming even more the beautiful, talented and compassionate women and men that God has designed and equipped each of you to be.

I was also greatly blessed and daily sustained by the kindness and collegiality of my friends and fellow professors, especially, Kukwoon Lee, Junmo Cho, Jeremy Knapp, and Nicholas Lantinga. Finally, I am most grateful to the one God designed especially to balance out all of my weaknesses and shortcomings – to my beloved wife, Sandy – absence does indeed make the heart grow fonder. To all who compose the community of teaching and learning at Handong, I dedicate this book with sure confidence in God's promise to continue to perfect the work that He has begun within you ~ a work that He will bring to completion in His day.

Preface

It is an honor and pleasure to write a preface for Cordell Schulten's *Life Abroad @ Handong*. The book is a collection of blog entries which he posted online for several years. *Cantos: A Literary and Arts Journal*, an annual magazine I edit at Missouri Baptist University, published some of those entries in its 2008 and 2010-13 issues. I suggested to Cordell many times that he should publish his blog posts as a book, so it is exciting to learn that he finally took time to complete a book manuscript.

Cordell and I have been close friends and colleagues for almost twenty years now. I first met him in the fall of 1999, when my family and I moved to St. Louis so that I could begin my full-time teaching career at MBU. Because I was born and grew up as a farm boy in South Korea and then lived in two agricultural states of Kansas and Nebraska for more than a decade, the size and speediness of a large metropolitan area overwhelmed me. In addition, I came to MBU with a work permit which allows foreign nationals short-term employment. This meant that I immediately needed to apply—and wait—for my green card, which involved many stressful legal steps and some sleepless nights. It was a dream come true to teach at a small Christian liberal arts college, yet the first couple of years at MBU were worrisome and anxiety-ridden.

Cordell played a key role in making my transition to a new chapter in life smooth and enjoyable. As a brother in Christ, he welcomed me, encouraged me, and supported me in both words and actions. Through his friendship, I gradually adapted to life at a new university and regained self-confidence as an immigrant. As fellow members of MBU's newly created Faith and Learning Committee, we organized in-house conferences on faith and learning, attended conferences at Baylor University and Michigan State University, and founded— along with some other colleagues—*Intégrité: A Faith and Learning Journal*, a nationally distributed academic journal that is now sixteen years old.

In the mid-2000s, Cordell became interested in going to South Korea to teach at Handong Global University, an American-style evangelical institution in Pohang, a port city across the sea from Japan. I supported his decision and gave him some tips—both solicited and unsolicited—on what to expect in Korea. I told him that he would be welcomed by Korean Christians who feel grateful for Americans bringing Christian faith to the Korean Peninsula at the turn of the twentieth century and for defending South Korea during the Korean War. I also told him that his engaging and passionate teaching style would clearly appeal to Korean students. Both of my predictions came true, and his years of service to Handong left an indelible mark on the university's history. His dedication to teaching and to his students is evidenced by the fact that he still communicates with his former students and hosts them at his home when they visit the United States.

In *Life Abroad @ Handong*, Cordell writes about his experiences while teaching American law at the university level in Korea. While reading his travel journals, readers will gain a unique understanding of living abroad, catching a glimpse of what it is like to work and serve in an unfamiliar environment and culture. His joy radiates throughout his writing, and he pays careful attention to every detail of his day. He describes everything—from the mundane differences between the two countries' food to the heartwarming interactions he had with his students.

Readers will find many of the episodes in this book both fascinating and instructive. One of Cordell's stories that I find most intriguing is his students' celebration of his birthday. He marvels at the generous, welcoming, and loving hearts of his students as they visited him at his home, waiting for the clock to strike midnight to surprise him with cards, gifts, and cake. This episode illustrates the ways in which Cordell's students thankfully reciprocate his genuine, sincere, and loving heart for them.

Perhaps the biggest impression from his experiences is the encouragement they provide us to live outside our comfort zones, motivating us to find and follow our own callings, to use our gifts, and to serve wherever God may call us. *Life Abroad @ Handong* offers readers the opportunity to follow Cordell's account of everyday events through which he follows his vocation and adjusts to living and serving in a new place. Those who read this book will be inspired by his sense of Christian calling, by his passion for serving others, and by his enthusiastic pursuit of cross-cultural understanding.

John J. Han, Ph.D.
Professor of English and Creative Writing
Chair, Humanities Division
Missouri Baptist University

Calling

1

Come and See

"Come and see what our God has done, what awesome miracles he does for his people!" (Psalm 66:5) What an invitation! Would you accept it? What if accepting meant traveling more than half-way around the world to a place you had never been before?

But, what if this invitation was issued through one of God's faithful servants? What if the Lord provided the funds to accept the invitation through a most remarkable set of circumstances in which His hand could not be denied? What if the invitation was actually a challenge to test whether you would, in fact, do what you had been teaching students to do for the past four years? What if, in so doing, you would have to leave a place a comfort, safety and security and take personal risks by going to where others are in deep need in an effort to help address some of those real, concrete needs in ways that embody the Gospel of Jesus Christ?

What if all the necessary paper-work for this journey sailed through both the U.S. government (providing you a renewed passport) and the Cambodian Consulate (granting you a visa) in less than 20 days? What if every barrier that might otherwise impede your way was removed, and you were left with this choice – a choice that would mean risking exposure to diminished personal comfort, safety and security?

Would you go? Would you come and see? You might be anticipating that I am going to say something like, "While I know most of you wouldn't, I jumped at the chance!" But that was indeed not the case. I doubted whether I should accept the invitation from the very beginning and even after all the roadblocks were cleared from my way, I still hesitated and haltered.

Had you asked me in January of 2003 if I would even be giving the slightest contemplation to serving on a project in East or Southeast Asia, I would have wondered from what planet you had just arrived. The entire continent of Asia was not even on the radar screen -- much less the remote country of Cambodia. But God has his way of "leading his own with his hand upon them." In the summer of 2003, at an academic conference in Chicago, I presented a paper on the topic "Some Limitations to Faith and Learning Integration." Immediately after my talk, a professor from Regent University by the name of Mike Schutt presented on a similar subject. My meeting Prof. Schutt led to an extended conversation over dinner that evening and later to an invitation from him to present at the Christian Scholars Symposium convened at the national conference of the Christian Legal Society in the fall of 2003. At that conference, my presentation was attended by two professors from Handong International Law School (HILS) in Pohang, Korea. Following the delivery of my paper, Prof. Hee Eun Lee and his colleague, Prof. Kuyper Lee, asked me to consider applying for a summer visiting professorship at their university. The following spring my application was accepted and in the summer of 2004, I taught a course on U.S. Antitrust Law at HILS in Pohang.

While teaching at HILS, I stayed in the campus apartment of Professor SK Lee -- one quite remarkable, 70-year-old, devoted follower of Christ. He had been instrumental in not only helping to establish Handong Global University in 1995, but also in founding their International Law School in 2001 when he served as the Law

School's first Dean. One early morning as the two of us walked around the perimeter of HGU's beautiful campus nestled in the foothills of the mountains above Pohang, Professor SK challenged me with a new opportunity that he was beginning to work on. I must admit, it sounded far-fetched – starting an evangelical Christian university where? – Cambodia? Isn't that a country still ruled by communists? What's that I remember from high school about the Khmer Rouge? Professor SK simply asked me, at that time, to begin praying about coming back and teaching again next summer (July 2005) at HILS and then the following summer (2006) in Cambodia, when he believed the new university would be up and running. How do you respond to a request like that coming from a devoted follower of Christ? How could I say that I wouldn't at least be willing to pray about it? So I did.

In October of 2004, my wife and I traveled to the national conference of the Christian Legal Society in McLean, Virginia. That year, however, the conference was held in conjunction with the international convocation of an organization called "Advocates International." Lawyers, judges and law professors, as well as law students, from over 100 countries were in attendance including Prof. S.K. Lee, Prof. Hee Eun Lee and another of their colleagues from HILS in Korea. In characteristic fashion, Prof. SK wasted no time in telling me about a project that was scheduled not for the summer of 2006, but for January 2005 in Siem Reap, Cambodia.

Then he said, "Come and see." That was the invitation that started my journey to Cambodia. When I returned from that first mission to Cambodia with my Handong University colleagues, many people asked me, "How was your trip?" The only phrase that I found to be a suitable response was: "Beyond phenomenal!" Not only was our team enabled, in three short weeks, to put together an initial proposal for the establishment of a new university (including a master site plan for the campus), we also were able to have several meetings with both provincial and central governmental officials. Each meeting went better than I had ever expected. We received the approval of the provincial authorities, and to top off the "awesome works" that we saw God performing there, the governor and his wife donated a tract of land measuring one kilometer by two kilometers (over 300 acres) for the site of the new university! At the conclusion of the international conference that our project group hosted in Siem Reap, Cambodia on 21 January 2005, I was asked to offer some brief remarks. Here is what I said:

"One generation ago this country endured three years, eight months and twenty days. The blood of the millions shed upon the multitude of killing fields of this land now cries out to us for healing. The world will not long remember what we say here, but it can never forget what the victims suffered here. May God grant this country a re-birth of freedom so that what was formally "The Killing Fields" may now become the Healing Fields – of the people, for the people and by the people of Cambodia. May the Spirit of Handong Global University be used by the grace of God and the love of Jesus Christ to help this new birth of healing peace come and prosper in and upon this beautiful land."

The next chapter will more fully recount my summer of teaching at HILS in 2004. I continued to stay in touch with Prof. S.K Lee during the intervening years. In the late summer of 2009, Prof. Lee invited me once again to come to Handong, this time as a professor of American Law in the University's undergraduate U.S. & International Law program of study. Those experiences fill the remaining chapters.

Way Points

2

Handong International Law School – Pohang, Korea

July 21, 2004

By God's good hand I arrived safe and sound here at the University late Wednesday evening (about 11pm Pohang time -- which would be about 9am Wednesday, St. Louis time). So about 28 hours of planes, trains, automobiles, buses all eventually brought me to my appointed destination. My flight out of St. Louis was delayed about 20 minutes which made my connection at O'Hare a bit more of an adventure, but the Korean mother and her two school-age kids that I met in St. Louis were a help. They were on their way to the same departure for Seoul. The 14 hour flight over passed through about 3 stretches of turbulence -- it felt like you were on a roller coaster -- but everything held together.

I was seated in row 62 about three rows from the very back of the plane, so I think the location in the tail tended to exaggerate the dips and drives. Needless to say, I did not get a whole lot of sleep -- maybe an hour here and there. Arrival in Seoul went smoothly, though. After making my way through Immigration and customs at Incheon International Airport, I went out to catch a shuttle bus over to Gimpo., the domestic airport. But, while I was waiting for the bus, some Korean "teenage-idol" came out of the doorway surrounded by four military guards and about 50 screaming 12 year old girls. I almost got push off the bus stop by the thronging fans, but the ruckus soon passed and I was able to catch my bus. When I got through the ticketing and baggage check-in at Gimpo Airport, I finally had a few moments to scrounge-up a meal. So where would I get my first meal in Korea? Much like our first meal in Ireland last year, I found a place called "Lotteria" that is like a McDonald's and ordered a cheeseburger and fries. The burger reminded me of a White Castle. Glad I only ordered one. After downing the burger and fries, I made my way through security and down to my departure gate. I still had about an hour to wait, so I went exploring around the concourse and found a food mart quick store that sold Haagen-Dazs ice cream bars.

Great! I could settle-down that White-Castle-like burger with the rich creaminess of Haagen-Dazs vanilla with chocolate and almonds. What a treat! It was a quick flight over from Seoul to Busan where I was picked-up by a taxi cab driver who drove me the last hour and a half up to Pohang and the university. I tried to sleep in the back of the taxi since my driver had the disturbing habit of driving very fast right up nearly on the bumper of the car ahead before jumping over to an adjacent lane to pass the slower car honking his horn all the way. Once again, needless to say, I didn't get much rest in the back of the taxi, but I did arrive safely.

I was met by Dean Hee Eun Lee who has been coordinating everything for my teaching term here. My housing is an apartment of one of the faculty members from the law school who is away from campus teaching in Kyrgyzstan (one of the former Soviet Republics in Central Asia), so I have a small three room apartment to myself. It is quite comfortable -- firm twin-sized (or a little smaller) bed. The shower, however, doesn't have a curtain, but that's the design in Korea, I'm told. The whole bathroom area (which isn't that big to begin with) is effectively the shower stall. There's a big drain in the middle of the room for the water. It's now about 12:30pm Thursday afternoon here, so that makes it 10:30pm Wednesday night in St. Louis. Dean Lee will be taking me to lunch soon and then to do a little shopping.

July 22, 2004

I'm taking a break from the student presentations in the Refugee Law class. They're very interesting, though. The Lord is opening my eyes to the rampant injustice and evil that is being done to people in many places of the world at this very moment. The first presentation set forth a case for genocide against the North Korean government for its systematic killing of babies born to women who had fled to China as refugees only to be forced into prostitution or raped and then sent back to North Korea where their newborn babies are killed or they are forced to have an abortion because the children are not "pure blood" Korean. It is challenging to meet young people who have a calling to give themselves in service to those who are so oppressed.

A year ago, Eric Enlow, an attorney I had met around 10 years before, emailed me asking about my change of careers from law practice to teaching. He had found me on the MBU website, I think. I corresponded with him once or twice and then didn't hear from him. When I arrived on Wednesday, Dean Lee told me that Eric is now on the faculty here. He and his wife and three kids moved over to the University about 5 months ago. What a small world! Once again I find that there are usually less than 3 degrees of separation in the Christian community. Sometimes, though, its pretty amazing the connections you discover especially as you see God working in the lives of others and even through you when you don't realize it. I think that is often when He does His most effective work in others (when we don't realize that he, in his grace, is using us for his purposes). I took a walk around campus at dusk. It was a good walk even though it was still quite hot and humid. The whole campus is 188 acres. (I think that is about a little more than 4x's the size of MBU) It's nestled in the hills above the city of Pohang, but on a clear day, you can see the East Sea. This is really an amazing place. The university only started in 1995 but the number and size of the buildings is remarkable. There are dormitories for about 2,500 students completely filled. Another 500 or so upper class or graduate students live in off-campus apartments. The international law school has about 75 students. There are even a few students here from the States and from other countries like Albania and China.

July 24, 2004

I think I'm living pretty much on adrenalin over here. My body clock is still in the process of adjusting to being awake when it thinks it should be asleep and then sleeping when I would normally be awake. Friday was a full and eventful day. After the student presentations, I was invited to a pizza lunch (well it looked pretty much like pizza, but don't ask me what all was on it, but it was a bunch of stuff). I met and spent some time talking with Mrs. Kim the Secretary General (head person in charge) of an NGO (Non-Governmental Organization) here in Korea called "Citizens Alliance." Their work is to assist refugees from North Korea and resettle them in the South. Most of them are women and children who have fled from North Korea up into China.

If they get caught by the Chinese authorities, they are sent back to North Korea (NK) and put in concentration camps. The NK calls them "re-education facilities" There is so much injustice and oppression of the ordinary people in NK. Most children are not provided with adequate food or health care. The death rate for children is astronomical. Mrs. Kim has many stories to tell of people her organization has helped. Even as we were talking, she received a call on her mobile phone from a North Korean refugee woman who had made it as far as Beijing, China. Mrs. Kim was trying to arrange for her and her daughter to be brought into South Korea. It's amazing the burdens of others that Mrs. Kim and her co-workers are bearing!! (Gal. 6:2 -- "...so fulfilling the law of Christ.") About 5:30 in the afternoon some of the law school faculty members and a few of the law students played basketball on one of the several courts near the University's student center. (the recreational facilities are phenomenal, too). I was invited to join in, so in spite of the heat and humidity (95 F) I rose to the challenge. My strength, though, was quickly drained. I played about 30 minutes (sitting out every 5 minutes or so to catch my breath). I think I even scored a basket or two, but I still need to improve on my set-shot form.

Around 9pm, Eric Enlow came by my apartment and we went out for an evening walk around the campus. We made two laps in about one hour talking all the way about our life experiences and how the Lord has been directing our families (his a young one, mine a seasoned one of nearly 26 years). Eric was intrigued to hear about all the different interests our kids have. Each one is unique. Each one is being formed by God in His time and by His ways -- into the person he has designed and is equipping them to be as they find their "flow" in life as they serve others.

After our walk, we made our way back to the Enlow's apartment. It's designed for a family so it must be about 3x's the size of the one I'm staying in. Same basic floor plan only each room is much bigger, and I think they have 3 bedrooms instead of just two. Eric's wife Danika greeted us and made some "cowboy coffee" for all to enjoy. They have friends that sent them real Colombian ground coffee from the States (you can't get that around here; all the coffee is the instant variety -- which shouldn't even be called coffee at all). Only problem is, they don't have a coffee maker let alone even an old-fashioned coffee pot. So, the way they make their brew is to cover the bottom of a sauce pan with about a quarter inch layer of ground coffee, pour in the water and boil for about 5-10 minutes. Then you let the grounds settle to the bottom of the pan and ladle out the coffee off the top into mugs to which are added the cream (whole milk) and sugar. Now that's one powerful cup of coffee!!!! I imagine it packed the caffeine of about 4-5 cups of QT's finest, so you might have suspected that we talked for a few more hours being as wired as we were --- wow!! The other little treat Danika shared was some dried sweet potato slices. Sort of like dried slices of fruit -- apricots, pineapple and banana. The Korean dried almost everything -- fruit, vegetables, beef, pork, all varieties of seafood -- fish, squid, shark and the list goes on to even more exotic stuff.

Saturday evening, Eric and his family hosted a wonderful meal with an assortment of Korean dishes (except the dog bit) for all three of us American visiting professor. Lynn Pace from Peacemakers Ministries in Montana arrived Saturday afternoon. She is staying in the apartment across the hall from mine (the building is like a four-family flat, with two apartments on the ground floor and two above) with Kathleen. Lynn is a Harvard Law grad and Kathleen is a graduate of Georgetown Law School in the Washington, DC area. Lynn was a theatre major in undergrad and loves to sing Broadway show tunes. Eric plays the mandolin. So we should have some interesting entertainment in the coming days.

July 26, 2004

It's now 8pm on Monday. I just concluded meeting with two students who have been talking to some of the students in my class and they have asked for my permission to allow them to join the class -- if Dean Lee also agrees then my class with grow to 8 students. (6 women, 2 men -- one from Mongolia, one from China and the other six from Korea) One of the students is not a believer. She came to Handong because she had heard that it was an international law school and she wants to go to the US to practice law. Some of the students are married and have children. They are all very respectful and dedicated to their studies. Many are still in the Law Library even now reading their cases for tomorrow's class.
The day began with devotions in the Moot Court Room attended by all the students and faculty members. The singing was great!

The Korean really loves to sing. Dean Lee gave the message from 2 Samuel on David as a model of servant-leadership. It was great. Prof. Won reported on the efforts of Mrs. Kim and the Citizen's Alliance. They were able to contact the UN and provide a means for the women in Beijing with her daughter to be transported safely to South Korea. If she had been caught in China, she would have been deported back to North Korea and imprisoned in a concentration camp for the rest of her life. She was delivered from that fate with her daughter too through the concerted efforts of both the people from Citizens Alliance and the professors here at Handong who made the contacts with the UN in Geneva by phone and fax all through out the afternoon and evening this past Friday. What a powerful testimony to the love of Christ in action to deliver the oppressed!!

After class, Dean Lee and a couple of the other full-time professors took the three of us visiting summer term prof's out to lunch at a very interesting sea-side restaurant. The building is designed to look like a giant patch of mushrooms. It sits high on a hillside overlooking the East Sea. The weather is a little cooler today; humidity is lower due to a breeze blowing in from the Sea. The sights were breath-taking! There were scenes that reminded me of the Wicklow Mountains in Ireland and others that reminded me of the Pacific Northwest coastline in Oregon and Washington and even some of the coastal areas around Bar Harbor, Maine -- plus in another area of the coast there is a great beach. Dean Lee told us to get down to the beach sometime this week, because next week begins the holiday season in Korea and the beaches will be packed with people. The food was pretty Western but prepared with a Korean flair. I had a rib eye steak (about 6 oz) in teriyaki sauce, though not as sweet as the teriyaki we get in the US. It came with 5 French fries neatly arranged in a cress-cross design, one small (very small) stalk of broccoli and two very small carrots. Thank the Lord for dessert! -- a one inch cubed piece of cake and a bowl of ice cream -- (you guessed it --- one small scoop) And all that for only 22,000 Won! The Dean was very gracious to treat us to such an elaborate meal -- 22,000 Won is not cheap -- it's about $20 US. It was a bit cramped. The speed and winding roads (some even gravel) made for another exciting ride. Upon returning to campus, I stopped into my office for a while. One of my students, Joshua Roh, came by and we talked for about 30 minutes. I had mentioned to my students in the morning class that I had a web page on the MBU website, and Joshua had gone to my web page and read my testimony and the article about my law school. I think I may be meeting with him regularly; he is very interested in serving the Lord and others through the practice of law. He is married and he and his wife have two young boys, one 5 and the other just about 4 months.

I probably should head back to my apartment and re-read the antitrust cases I'll be teaching tomorrow. I also put together my sermon outline notes and sent it over to the Korean-English church where I've been asked to preach this Sunday. All in all it was yet another exciting and challenging day. Each day I'm finding out more about Handong and I'm even more impressed with the vision and mission of the faculty and students here. The University's motto is "Why Not Change the World?" and with the people I'm privileged to meet and get to know and serve with here -- it is quite clear -- they will be changing the World because they already are doing it. Life is so short. We need to live purposefully everyday to the fullest, in His will, by His grace, according to His Word and promise and through His Spirit -- loving others; serving others -- and so glorifying our Father!

July 27, 2004

Today marks the end of my first week here at Handong. It is hard to believe I'm one-third of the way through my visiting professorship this summer. But time speeds ever on its way – all the more reason to make the most of each moment. The second day of class went well. One of the two new students was allowed to join my class -- Mr. Mark Kim from Korea. He has a LLB from the undergraduate school of law at Handong University and speaks English well.

I took a long walk around 5:10am along a trail that leads through the forested area of the campus along a ridge of several hills. I found a recently fallen pine sapling that made for a sturdy walking staff. After hiking the trail through the woods, that led, by the way, alongside two burial sites -- large mounds of earth with a small stone an the foot to mark the grave, I then took the long walk all the way around the campus outer drive and down the main road to the entrance. I heard a lot of coo-coo birds along the way and saw magpies flying through the trees. I also found a couple of rocks that will make great (but small) memorial stone replicas of the main entrance monument for the university.

Class went very well today. It is moving much slower than the pace I had anticipated, but I know it is much more important to make sure the students are understanding the topics we are discussing than to just rush through a bunch of material they won't be able to comprehend. They read and comprehend English, however, much better than they can speak English, so their slowness in speech does not mean that they are not comprehending what they are reading or what I'm saying in class. In fact, judging from the questions they pose, they are all extremely bright -- as you might expect from law students.

Well, I'm finishing up my office hours this afternoon. Some of the students from my class come by to talk about the class and ask questions. Prof. Enlow has offered to take me and Lynn into Pohang to shop at the LG (Korean Schnucks). I want to get a dozen eggs, a half-gallon of milk, some more yogurt and maybe even some pork sausage or bacon for my breakfasts.

July 30, 2004

I've just come from a great conversation with one of the full-time prof's here, Tarik Radwan (his father was Egyptian and his mother was from California) He is quite American and I've found that we share some life experiences. He is 43 and came to personal faith in Christ in his high school years. We talked of our experiences in high school and thereafter. He had read my brief testimony of the time our family spent during my law school years. It was a good talk.

Well, this evening marks just about the half-way point in my challenging teaching adventure here in Korea. It has been great thus far, but I must say that I am very tired and feeling worn-down. Last evening I mentioned that Prof Pace and I had been taken out by one of my students, Joshua Roh, and his family to the Pohang City Park for a festival. The name of the park is "Sunrise Park" because it is located down on the seaside and you can get a wonderful view of the sunrise in the mornings. There was an arts festival going on with a really cute puppet show (with Muppet-like puppets) for the young children of the old story "Little Red Riding Hood" but all in Korean. It was very funny and every once and a while you could pick-up on what the characters were saying, like "O Grandmother, what big eyes you have!"

On the main stage in the park amphitheater that looked out over the sea, a theater group of actors put on a musical version of Shakespeare's comedy "Twelfth Night." Imagine music styles from a Frank Sinatra style on the one hand to a "Rap" version of a song on the other hand -- plus every thing from Michael Bolton/Kenny G - style singing and playing and Michael Jackson - style dance routine in between. And oh yes, I took some pictures. My student Joshua also took some pictures so I'm hoping to be able to send you. We returned to campus about 11:30pm. So, I made it to bed by 12:15am and pretty much went sound to sleep -- UNTIL .

. . . . . around 3am I was awaken by the lights being turned on in the apartment and a lot of noise being made. Dean Hee Eun Lee had not told me that my host -- the professor (Prof. S.K. Lee) who lives in the apartment where I was staying -- would be returning this week. He had just gotten off the bus from Seoul after flying in from a week's visit in Kyrgyzstan (located north of Afghanistan in Central Asia). He was there with several other law professors, judges and lawyers meeting with the judges of the Kyrgyzstan Supreme Court and learning about the legal system that has been developing there since the down-fall of the Soviet Union in 1989. Before then, this country had been dominated by the Soviet Communists. Now they free to govern themselves and they are open to learning from and hoping to adopt more democratic-style laws and government structures to ensure equal justice under law to the people of their country. Prof. S.K. was quite wired as he told me more stories about his trip. I only lasted about 30 minutes before I started dozing off and needed to go back to bed.

My alarm, however, went off (as it does each morning) at 6:10am. So, I pulled myself out of bed and into the shower. Since Joshua had fixed the gas range top yesterday, I was able to fix those scramble eggs I had been longing for. They were very good, but I missed having a little black pepper to sprinkle over them. (The Korean use a lot of red pepper, but black pepper is quite a bit scarcer in my limited experience.) It was, though, a fortifying breakfast. I was able to make it and get ready for class (shower, shaved and dressed) before Prof. Lee awoke and came out of his bedroom. We talked for a short while. He showed me some of the wonderful gifts that he was given including two very elaborate black wool robes with intricate gold embroidery that the Kyrgyzstan Supreme Court Justices wear in court. I headed over to the Law School building and did my morning readings (also still preparing for the sermon I'm to give this Sunday at the Evangelical (English-speaking) church in Pohang City this Sunday. Class went well. My students are well-prepared, although like me, after a full week of classes every morning from 9am-12noon, we were all very,

very worn-out. I told them a few "war stories" from my law practice years, including the case I tried for Dennis Nagy against the Highway Department that was appealed up to the Missouri Supreme Court where I presented an oral argument. They were quite impressed and went searching after class for the opinion of the court in the Nagy v. Bangert Bros. Construction Co. case that is reported in the Southwestern Court Reporter volumes in the library.

After class, all three of the visiting summer professors were invited along with Prof. Eric Enlow by Prof. S.K. Lee to lunch. Prof. S.K. regaled us with more stories of his recent travels and the open doors God has made available to serve the people of Kyrgyzstan through the development of that country's laws and legal system. Prof Lee took us to another seaside restaurant. This one closer to Pohang. We sat at a window table overlooking the sea. The food was good. Sort of a western menu. I had spaghetti and meat sauce (but it clearly had a Korean flair). I was full, though. And yet, I still accepted Prof. Lee's offer of dessert -- chocolate ice cream and green tea -- very soothing. Back to campus by about 2:15pm and up to my office for a short bit of work. Then back over to the apartment where I took a long nap and I'm feeling a little better now. Well, time to say good night from me, but good morning to you. Hope you are able to read this shortly after you arrive at your office Friday morning. Tomorrow, we are all going on a very special tour to the City of Gyeongju -- the ancient city of Buddhist Temples and the Tombs of Kings and Rulers of ancient Korea. I will take a lot of pictures

August 01, 2004

Sunday, 5:20pm. I've just shortly returned from the local church services where I had the privilege to preach today. Prof. Enlow is their regular English-language preacher in the 2pm English worship service. The congregation was very warm and responsive. Eric's wife, Danika, commented to me after the service that the message (from John 21 "Jesus Recharges Disillusioned Disciples") was very timely for many in their congregation who she knew personally to be struggling with issues about personal calling and direction and were in need of encouragement. I was very encouraged to hear that from her! The Enlow's took me shopping on the way back to campus and a brought some fried chicken at the local LG super store (like a Schnuck's). Man, was it good. It reminded me of Poppy Reed's standard response to my mom's inquiry "What would you like for Sunday dinner, Poppy? ---- "Oh, I don't know . . . . . Chicken'll be fine." It sure was fine this afternoon. Helps to fill-in where the Korean cuisine comes up a bit lacking some days.

Yesterday, we spent the day touring in Gyeongju -- the city of the ancient kings of Korea. Several of the students traveled with us, all in an extended van. The driver was Joseph Kim, a 3d year law student. His wife is a physician's assistant in practice already and Joseph is just about to finish law school and then they hope to travel to the US for Joseph to do additional studies at an American law school in an LLM program. He shared his testimony with me as we drove along the highway (very nice wide and well-maintained highway, much like our interstates) from Pohang to Gyeongju, about an hour's drive up from the coastal area to the mountains of South Central Korea.

Joseph was born into a Buddhist family. In fact, his mother's brother (his uncle) is among the most well-respected Buddhist monks and scholars in all of Korea. When he was in high school, though, he had many friends who were Christians. On one occasion when he was in a very difficult situation, he promised that he would one day go to a Christian church. Several years later, during his university studies, I think, he was reminded of the promise he had made and he went with some Christian friends to a church. Later he had a vision that confronted him with the reality of life after death, and he was very afraid. He asked God for a sign and shortly afterward during a family gathering where he, as the oldest son in his family, was leading a memorial for the family's deceased ancestors, a sign was given to his entire family. Joseph was convinced that Jesus was indeed God himself, not just a great teacher, and he came to faith in Him as his Savior. He is still young in the faith but is studying God's word and trusting that God will continue to nurture his faith as he grows stronger and stronger.

I think the Koreans love to tell long, long, long, stories. That's been my experience, while sharing a meal at a restaurant, while riding in vans, while riding on buses, while standing half-asleep in my apartment when my host returned from a trip -- in nearly every conceivable situation, a Korean will be happy to tell you his life's story. Maybe they also enjoy practicing their English and very much appreciate having an American ear to suggest a better way to express their thoughts in English. We had departed campus Saturday morning around 10am, so we were pulling into the large parking lot of the first major site in Gyeongju -- it was Buddha's Country Temple -- a very large Buddhist temple complex with a monastery adjoining the temple grounds.

It was breath-taking in many respects -- I was particularly taken by the order and arrangement of the buildings and colonnades. Korean/Buddhist architecture seeks to harmonize man-made structure with their natural surroundings -- and here there were some awesomely beautiful natural surroundings of pine tree covered mountain-sides, flowing brooks and flowering shrubberies. The footprint of the buildings (if you just took a picture of the lay-out from directly above the area -- looks very much like the arrangement of the abbey's we toured through in Wales. Remember Tintern Abbey in the Wye River Valley of South Wales? The lay-out of the buildings, including the cloister walks, of this Buddhist monastery was nearly the same. The building structures were uniquely Korean -- mainly constructed of pine logs and painted in colorful decorations in great, great detail. We must have spent nearly 3 hours walking the grounds and talking to an English-speaking guide who told us the entire history of the temple complex and was able to answer our many questions. Later, we drove a short way to a Korean restaurant where we had a traditional meal of beef and vegetables simmered in a skillet over an open gas fire on each of our tables. There were the usual innumerable and indecipherable side-dishes -- I stuck to the vegetable ones and stayed clear of the ones with fish parts, etc. My facility with chopsticks is still in need of a great deal of improvement, but oh well, it means I eat less during the time spent at the table since most of the food drops off my chopsticks before I get them to my mouth.

Following lunch, we found a few shops and I picked up a couple more souvenirs. Trying to decide who of you all will get what is a tough go; I may end-up laying all the goods on the kitchen table when I get home and letting you choose for yourselves. There is some really cool stuff and not that expensive either. Joseph and another student Kyu Tae helped me bargain with one shop keeper over a beautiful calligraphy scroll that had been hand painted and sealed by the monks in the monastery. Yes, as you might imagine, I did end up buying it. It will adorn the wall of my office when I return. It's somewhat like my scroll that I got when I was studying martial arts in high school.

After our shopping spree, we loaded up the van again and headed up higher in the mountains to the most famous Buddha grotto in all of Korea (and I think in a large part of East Asia). It is like a cave, but it was hand-carved by the monks who had returned to Korea after studying with monks in northern India and China. There are a lot of caves with Buddha's in that part of central Asia, but in Korea, there are no naturally occurring caves, so the monks carved out the granite cave and placed the large (must be 25-30 feet tall) granite Buddha in the cave (maybe they just carved the Buddha out of the rock they had carved to make the cave. It was quite impressive. There is also another small monastery next to the grotto. I looked through the gateway into the inner court and saw a monk in the distance. When he noticed people outside the gate, he made a slow but deliberate retreat to the solitude of the monastery cloister. The view from up on these mountains was spectacular!!!! It was almost clear enough to see all the way back about 40km (20 miles or so) to the coast and see the East Sea. A storm was brewing, though, so the distance was a bit obscured. The way up to the grotto was about a 30 walking on a very well maintained and level mountain path. The terrain, though, reminded me of hiking the Big Piney Trail in Southern Missouri. The rock formations, mainly granite protrusions, were very much like the Elephant Rocks down near Hahn State Park and farther south near Fredericktown and Arcadia Valley Bible Camp. I took two rolls of pictures during the entire day of touring. It was a thrilling, but exhausting day! We headed back around 6, taking a drive around the city of Gyeongju to see some of the many other sites that we just did not have time to stop and tour.

August 03, 2004

It's Tuesday afternoon about 3:15pm here at Handong (so 1:15am in St. Louis Monday night/Tuesday morning). Monday was another full day. We start the week with the entire law school -- students and professors -- gathering in the Courtroom for a time of devotions. One of the full-time prof's here, Michael Whitman, shared the message from Ephesians 4 -- emphasizing our need to endeavor to keep the unity of the Spirit in the bound of peace and how every believer is connected to one another in the community of the Body of Christ and is dependent upon one another for our growth and fruitfulness.

Class is going well, although I'm not covering half of the cases I had planned to cover. I just take more time for me to communicate the legal concepts of Antitrust Law -- and they are not easy concepts to grasp, even if English is the student's first language. It also takes a lot of time for me to understand what my students are saying. They can read and write English very well, but when it comes to speaking it, their native accents and difficulty in pronouncing English vowel and consonant sounds, create barriers to the ease of communication. It's truly an on-going lesson in patience on both sides of the table. I spent the remainder of the afternoon and early evening preparing for my class and beginning to work-up the examination questions I will present to my students at the end of this week. I headed back to the apartment around 8 or so. I had planned to do a bit more work after my supper, but when I got some fried chicken from the refrigerator and heated in the microwave, I was quite full and not so much in the mood for more work. So, I enjoyed a dessert of whipped bananas (I had purchased a bunch of bananas from the store and they were starting to go bad -- turn dark; when Prof. S.K. Lee saw them in the refrigerator, he warned me not to let them go to waste!) --so I stirred up five small bananas with some milk and made myself a shake. After that, I was feeling sleepy (I think it was the milk and the potassium from the bananas), so I turned in early (around 9:15 after watching a bit of the news on CNN and then some tennis on one of the cable sports network)

And then . . . you guessed it . . . . . IT HAPPENED YET AGAIN!!!!!!!! This time, Prof. S.K. Lee had invited Kathy McKee and Lynn Pace over to his apartment to visit with them. This must have been around 10:30pm or so, I was fast asleep in my bedroom with the door just opened a crack. At first, I thought I was dreaming when I heard the voices of women in the apartment, but then I realized that Prof. Lee had guests -- at the time I didn't know who, and decided it would be better for me not to walk out in the living room in only my pj bottoms. So I just turned over, and went back to sleep. When I awoke early this morning (around 5:10am), I tried to get out of the apartment without waking SK, but to no avail. He was up and accusing me of being out very late the night before. When I explained that I had been asleep in my room the entire evening, he became very apologetic since he and Lynn and Kathy had been talking and laughing quite loudly, although, I told him, it did not disturb my sleep (---well, not that much). Prof. S.K. then asked if he could come along on my walk, since he had not yet had any time alone with me to get to know me better. On our walk, he asked me about how God had been leading in my life and in the lives of our family. He was encouraged to here about our experiences on mission trip in England, Ireland and Wales. Prof. S.K. shared with me his vision for Handong Int'l Law School and how his role here at Handong has been completed. Now, at the age of 70, he believes God is directing him to help in the establishment of sister universities in Kyrgyzstan and in Cambodia. Handong already has a joint program up and running with a university in Mongolia, and now the University is trying to establish similar programs in Cambodia and Kyrgyzstan.

When we made it around the campus on our walk, Prof. S.K. showed me the memorial tree that had been planted by the charter class of Handong International Law School in 2002. The University has been operating since 1995, but the Law School where I am teaching this summer is only in its third year of operation. He also showed me a tree that was planted in his honor by his law students to celebrate and commemorate Prof. S.K.'s service as a founding professor at the Law School. After breakfast, Prof. S.K. invited me to a morning Bible study that he attends regularly with Professor Ezra Kim from the University's architecture program and Prof. Michael Whitman -- who had shared the devotional message Monday morning for the law school. They were studying the passage in Heb 12 about accepting the Lord's discipline as a father disciplines his sons -- showing his love and care for their growth and fruitfulness. They started their time together with a hymn. We sang "Jesus, I my Cross Have Taken, all to leave and follow thee . . ." Prof. S.K. and Ezra sang in Korean and Michael and I sang in English --- cool!

Then, I was off to the law school for class. My students and I made it through 3 cases in our 3 hours together this morning. That's good progress! Shortly after morning classes, Prof. SK Lee asked all three of us visiting prof's from American to come with him across campus so he could introduce us all to the President of the

University, President Young Gil Kim. He has quite an office! I was impressed that his conference table is round! The chairs are all leather and overstuffed – sort of felt like you might be at King Arthur's Round Table. He gave us each a copy of a book he had written that shares his personal testimony and the story of the founding of the university! A true account of the on-going work of God here in Korea that is touching many places in Asia.

August 4, 2004

It's about all I can do just to reach up and stroke the "exclamation mark" key. I sure don't feel exclamatory this evening. In fact, I am just about worn-out. I feel drained of energy and drained of enthusiasm. I've been here now two whole weeks, and I must be honest . . . I am so looking forward to getting home. The schedule here is so rigorous . . . or maybe I'm just pushing myself too hard.

Last evening, as I mentioned yesterday, I was invited over to Lynn and Kathy's apartment for a home-cooked Korean meal by one of Lynn's students, the young man, Kyu Tae Lim. He's the fellow that was one of our guides this past Saturday when we toured at Gyeoung-Ju. Kyu Tae studied in the states at both Oral Roberts University in Tulsa, Okla. where he earned a BA in Business and a MA in Practical Theology. He also studied for about a year at Trinity Evangelical University up near Chicago -- all in all, he spent about 7 years in the states. Now, he's back home studying law at HILS (that's what everyone around here calls "Handong International Law School"). He's just a first-rate, all-around great guy and quite fun to be with. He prepared bulgolgi for us -- that's a beef dish with a marinade that is absolutely delicious. We all used chopsticks, some more efficiently than others.

Around the table we enjoyed a great time of fellowship as Lynn, Kathy and I each traded "war stories" from our years in the practice of law. It became one of those "can you top this" rounds of story-telling. I regaled them with stories of my "Master Dang" Vietnamese Meditation Cult case, and the deposition where I had to represent the dentist from South Carolina who had been charged (and found not guilty) of murdering his wife in the shower of their Hilton Head Island condominium. Kyu Tae just sat there and absorbed the evening. He heard and saw some American lawyers tell stories on themselves that revealed that the practice of law alone, though it can be quite life-consuming at times, can in the end, never make a person whole. It takes the love of family -- spouse, children, the fellowship of a local gathering of fellow followers of Christ, and most importantly of all -- a growing and deepening, personal relationship with the very person of Christ Himself. We concluded the evening with a time of prayer that was capped-off with the Doxology -- "Praise God from Whom All Blessings Flow . . ."

I couldn't get to sleep, though. I tossed and turned from 10 until nearly 12:30am, I think. Finally, I must have dozed off and then woke-up just before 5am. I was up and needing to get out of the apartment, so I took the long, nearly hour-length, walk around campus and down to the main entrance on the road to Pohang. It was a bit hazy, and the humidity felt like it was going to be another scorcher --- and it was, somewhere in the mid-90's F. I got back to the apartment, showered and ate a bite of breakfast. The propane stove is still not working (this is the third day) so that Texas--style omelet I've been planning to make, ever since I bought the eggs, green and red pepper, onion and (since ham as we know it in St. Louis, or even in Sheffield, England, for that matter, is unknown in these parts of East Asia) some canned SPAM -- that omelet will still have to wait. Maybe sometime tomorrow the service man will come and refill our propane tank -- one can hope and pray. So, getting back to this mornings breakfast, I had cereal with strawberry yogurt. Not bad, but it was no Texas Omelet. After my personal quiet time, I went over to the office for a short time, picked up your email from Tuesday morning your time, and will the burst of energy I always get from receiving an email from you, no matter how short, I was charged for the day. I headed back across campus to the Bible Study with Prof. S.K. Lee, Pastor Ezra and Prof. Whitman -- well Pastor Ezra never made it before I had to leave at 8:50am, but the three of us had an encouraging time -- we sang "A Mighty Fortress is Our God" together and read from Psalm 55 -- discussed spiritual warfare and the deep pain we feel when those closest to us (see Psalm 55:12-14) betray us -- are unfaithful to our trust. Prof. Lee asked for prayer for a major project that the law school faculty is working on for the Korean government.

I had to make a quick traverse back to the law school building and up to class to make it before 9am, but to my surprise, I found that my students are getting quite weary also. Only two of the seven were in class on time. It took the others nearly another 15 minutes to make it in. They are a real good group of students though. I realized they were worn-out, and they could sense that I was not as energetic as I had been the first week of class. Every once and a while the adrenalin still would kick-in, but it would only last for a few minutes, and then I was back to my weary self.

Well, after a lunch of micro waved beef and vegetable curry over rice back at the apartment, I trudged back up to my office (remember the law school classrooms and faculty offices are all on the fourth floor of the academic building that houses the law school, and there is no elevator -- mind you, there are several handicapped parking spaces in the parking lot outside, BUT inside, is there any elevator to aid the wheel-chair bound, or the weary laden visiting American professor who is about to drop from exhaustion -------- no. Up to my office to meet with one of my students, and then to write the examination that I will hand-out tomorrow at the end of class. The students will then come with their notes and research and write their examination answers in class Friday -- the final day of the session. Will I be so glad when that day is here!!!!

I'm sure the fact that I only got about 4 hours of somewhat restful sleep last night is the main reason I feel so down right now, but I still need to give some more thought and prayer to a devotional message that I've been asked to deliver Thursday morning for our final chapel time here with all the law students in the summer session. I thinking about that old hymn, "Sometimes a Light Surprises the Christian while he sings, it is the Lord who rises with healing in His wings; when comforts are declining, He grants the soul again, a season of clear shining to cheer him after rain." Well, we haven't had but one day of physical rain around here, but I feel like a dreary raining day in my soul this evening, so I'm trusting he'll give that "season of clear shining"

August 05, 2004

Thursday has come to a close for me (it's now 8:55pm) and will soon be beginning for you there in St. Louis. This day has been encouraging and recharging. Thanks for your prayers. I was asked by Dean Hee Eun Lee to share again during devotions. I presented a "readers' digest version" of my message from John 21, yet it seemed to challenge me even as I spoke to the students and few other prof's that attended this morning's chapel time. I reminded them that the Lord has a special call on each of our lives and that we need to reflect upon that call each day, and seek Christ's presence to reaffirm us in our call.

Next, I shared about the importance of examining ourselves daily to honestly access who or what is the love of our life. I suggested that we can do this my frankly answering for ourselves before the Lord three questions: Who or what did I spend time with yesterday (in the past 24 hours); who or what did
I listen to yesterday? And who or what did I think about yesterday? The answer to those questions is what (or who) we truly love? We may say we love Jesus or that we love another person, but did we spend time with him? Listen to him? Think about him? Finally, I reminded them that Jesus points us (as he did

with Peter in John 21) to the end of our life here on earth, and challenges us with this question: What will be the end of your life? By what kind of death will you glorify God? I challenged them with the words of Jim Elliot (with my slight paraphrase) -- "he is no fool who risks what he cannot keep, because he has already been given what he can never risk losing."

At the end of chapel, Dean Hee Eun Lee presented the three of us summer prof's with law school polo shirts as a gift of their appreciation and Prof. S.K. Lee offered the closing prayer seeking God's blessing on all of us as we complete the summer term today and tomorrow. My students came ready to class for the last day of lecture/discussion. We were able to cover two final cases, including the case of Morgan v. Ponder -- that the antitrust case I worked on back in 1987-1989 at Lewis & Rice with Jim O'Brien. I showed them the appellate brief that we wrote for the 8th Circuit US Court of Appeals that won a reversal of the jury verdict that had been entered after the week-long trial down in Cape Girardeau, Missouri. I told a few "war stories" from the case which my students enjoyed very much. We also took several pictures of the class that I'll have to show you when I return.

Lunch was served at the law school as SK Lee and several of the students that had accompanied him last week on the trip to Kyrgyzstan gave a report with a PowerPoint picture slide show. Kyrgyzstan is in Central Asia, north of India and west of China. It has a mountain range that reminded me of the Grand Tetons in Wyoming. Absolutely gorgeous!! Later in the afternoon I was to be given a very special blessing. One of the people from the Bukbu Church where I preached last Sunday and will preach again this Sunday, came to campus and picked me up to take me to Pohang so that I could visit Elder Kim Jin Won, one of the church elders who is also the principal of a very prestigious private elementary school. He is also a professional calligrapher (one who paints/draws traditional Korean and Chinese script characters and makes scrolls and paints water-color paintings) -- in short, he is a very accomplished and well-known artist in Korea. While I watched (and took a lot of pictures) he painted for me a traditional Korean scene and then hand-painted Korean letter characters of the verse from Gal. 6:2 "Bear one another burdens and so fulfill the law of Christ." It is a priceless gift, a treasure!! Caleb, especially will love this! I will buy a special packing tube on the University bookstore tomorrow so that I can transport it on the flights back without it getting damaged.

Shortly after my friend from the church drove me back to the Handong campus, I met up again with Lynn, Kathy, Prof. SK and Dean Hee Eun Lee and his wife Grace. They took us to a special restaurant that specializes in tofu -- just the place for Caleb, Michaela and Hannah! It was called "Tofu Village" We had tofu appetizers, tofu soup, tofu stew, tofu entrees of every kind and style -- some firm, some soft, with a variety of flavors -- oh yes, some cold, some hot and some lukewarm. I ate a lot of rice and found one dish that tasted like potatoes -- that was my mainstay -- although some of the tofu dishes were okay. The spicy stew is still rumbling around in my stomach -- hope it will let me sleep tonight. The meal was topped off with some green tea -- very soothing.

August 06, 2004

Today was the last day of class -- examination day. Most students completed the writing of their exams in about 2 hours or so. Two of my students (two of my better students) however, took the entire 3 hour exam period. All wrote fairly well, two excelled though. After a quick bite of lunch (Ramon noodles over at the apartment) I spent the better part of the afternoon reading and marking exams. About 4:30 I made it back to the apartment for that nap you have been urging me to take. This evening, Lynn and I and a student, Hector (from Albania) took the university bus into town. I wanted to start my readjustment to western culture process -- so we ate at the McDonald's in downtown Pohang. And, they are right. A cheeseburger and fries at McDonald's in Pohang,

Korea tastes just like a cheeseburger and fries in Fenton, Missouri, USA. What a wonder of modern culture!?!?   After the fine dining at Mickey D's, we walked a few blocks down to Jukto Market -- the open market bazaar in the city centre. Lynn found a few things she wanted to get -- some dishes for an authentic Korean place setting for two -- and we found a coffee maker for the Enlow's. We wanted to give them as a gift expressing our appreciation for their kindnesses to us. Danika and her kids have been dropping off little care-packages about every other day to surprise us. This morning is was a half-dozen Dunkin Donuts that they picked up for us in town. We caught the 9:45pm bus from the city centre back to campus. Its now 11:40pm here. It's been a pretty long day, so I'll close. Tomorrow several of the 1L's are taking us to Pusan (about 2 hours south of here). Pusan is the third largest city in Korea, so we should have some sights to see and experiences to remember. I'm scheduled to preach again at Bukbu Church this Sunday afternoon. Prof. S.K. Lee is in Seoul for the weekend to attend a wedding, so I have the apartment to my self once again. I hope that will mean a night of un-interrupted sleep. I could sure use it.

August 07, 2004

This evening, Lynn, Kyu Tae, Sam and Carrie and I are in Busan. We departed campus around 11:30am and the drive down took more than the 1 1/2 hours that Kyu Tae had anticipated. This is the busiest weekend of the summer season, so there are a lot of people driving down to Busan. It has one of the biggest and longest beaches in all of Korea, sort of like the Ft. Lauderdale, Florida of Korea. We made it into downtown along the breach front drive about 3pm or so. It took a long time just to find parking spot. Then we walked the length of the beach sidewalk (not down on the sand) because the beach itself was literally packed with people. You had asked a few days ago where all the people are in this very crowded country -- I think they were then and are definitely today down at Busan's breach. There is also a festival going on with a lot of stages set up for musical performances -- some where hopping and the big one was hold a rehearsal for a dance contest that must be going on down there now. Around 5pm we drove farther south. Kyu Tae wanted to show us a special lighthouse that is one of the landmarks of Busan Harbor. They have a big bridge across the harbor that looks like a mini Golden Gate Bridge. We had dinner at a traditional Korean restaurant -- I enjoyed the grilled rib steak strips. It was very tasty and for once I was able to order enough to fill me up. After dinner we drove around a park area where the lighthouse is located. The problem was we drove up the wrong way on a one-way drive through the park. Once we made it to the top of the cliff, there was a restaurant with enough parking places so we could turn around. We got lost again trying to find the motel where Kyu Tae had made us reservations. We finally just stopped along the street and Kyu Tae called the motel and they sent someone over to where we were parked. He then drove us back to the motel. We had missed the side street where we needed to turn-in and because there we so many one-way streets, it took this driver about 15 minutes to drive around to just get us back a couple of blocks to the motel. We got up to our rooms about 11pm and I wanted to send you this note. Tomorrow morning, we need to take Lynn by the airport and then head back up to Pohang so I can get to campus and change for church services at Bukbu where I will be preaching in the afternoon.

August 08, 2004

This last full day in Korea is now quickly coming to a close. These have surely been, in one way, some of the fullest days of my life thus far, but in other, deeper ways, they have undoubtedly been my most incomplete. How I have so very much missed you. You would love this place -- there is so much construction going on every where!!! :-) More than the building and places, though, the people of Korea -- of Handong, of Pohang, of Gyeongju, and even of Busan this weekend -- have proved to be so friendly, hospitable, respectful, and hungering for God's word and a sense of responding to His call on theirs lives!

The trip back this morning from Busan was, without question, one of my most pressing challenges of the entire three weeks here. Had I understood just how far we were to travel, and just how much traffic there would be on the highways during this weekend -- the height of the summer holiday season for the folks here, and just how much time we would end up spending cramped-up in our mini-van, I would most likely have regretfully, yet respectfully, decline the students find offer to treat us to a weekend, whirl-wind tour of the "Fort Lauderdale" of Korea. We departed the motel in downtown Busan around 8:15am and were able to make it (with only one wrong turn that resulted in back-tracking -- unlike Saturday night, when it seemed as though we were driving around in circles for at least an hour) -- we made it to the airport by 8:40am and got Lynn unloaded (all four of her big bags -- and Caleb thought I traveled heavy --) and into the terminal to wait in the Northwest Airlines/Asiana Airline check-in line. It finally opened a little after 9am and Lynn was chosen by the security guards to be the object of a complete -- that's every bag-- opened search through every item, take out nearly everything from the bags -- security check. We stood with her through the entire ordeal, and then saw her off down the line to get her boarding pass and then to the next security check-point.

Like Ezra in the OT traveling back from Persia to Jerusalem, I know God's good hand will bring me safely to my appointed destination in His perfect time. Well -- getting back to my story from today, after seeing-off Lynn at the Busan-Gimhae International Airport, we loaded back up in the van, Sam driving, Kyu Tae serving as navigator, and I took up my seat in the second row middle so I had a good view of the road ahead. Breakfast had only been a roll and a small orange-juice and then a rather weak cup of coffee, so my stomach wasn't in the greatest of shape for travel, but then, we didn't do much traveling on the highway through Busan -- average speed was about 10-15 mph -- local travelers returning back to their homes from a weekend at the Big Beach. We encounter our first major stoppage due to an auto accident just after passing through the first toll gate beyond Busan. We were delayed about 30 minutes, but then about half-way along the 78 kilometer trip (32 miles or so), we came to a dead-stop in a long line of traffic that seemed to stretch ahead us as far as we could see. It ended-up being a nearly 10 km long traffic jam. So needless to say, the trip that was supposed to have taken us about 2 hours, ended-up taking almost 4 hours to complete. By the time we were driving into the Pohang area I was feeling more than a little "green." I was sure my little breakfast wasn't going to stay down, and by this point Kyu Tae had taken over driving and was doing his best to make-up some of the time we had lost in the traffic jams. My heart appreciated his conscientiousness, but my stomach kept saying "could you just please slow down and stop making such abrupt stops and starts! Thankfully the Lord kept my stomach in one piece, but when we finally made it to campus and they dropped me off in front of the guest house, I nearly collapsed on the steps up to Prof. SK's apartment.

I made it in, turned on the AC full-blast and dropped into bed for 15 minutes -- I felt liked I had just gotten off a four-hour "ride" on the infamous Six Flags "Highland Fling". I didn't know how I was going to manage a shower, shaving and a bite of lunch before throwing on my suit and heading out with Prof. Eric Enlow and another Prof. from Korea to preach at The Joyful Church. The only, only way I can explain what happened to me in the next 30 minutes -- a complete "healing transformation" -- is by the fact that I knew you had been and were praying for me. I couldn't do it! But, by His grace and strength -- that is genuinely, authentically made complete in the midst of our utter weaknesses -- it happened.

We arrived at Joyful Church in downtown Pohang a little before 2pm, just enough time to get two pieces of toast and a cup of iced coffee down me, and then up the elevator to the fourth floor where the English language service had just begun. The worship team was leading in the song "I want to know you more" and then "I'm coming back to the heart of worship, and it's all about you, Jesus." How my heart and soul was ministered to by those songs, by 2:30 it was time for me to preach from 2 Corinthians 11:16-33 and I knew I had just experienced a little of what Paul had written about of his own ministry when he said "I am constantly on the go" and "if I am to boast, I will boast of those things that show my weaknesses." The message was well-received. Many of the folks came-up and spoke with me. We also to a great picture of nearly the entire congregation of the English-speaking service gathered around me. Elder Woo handed me another envelope like the one I had been given last week. They are such a gracious group of sincere believers! Many in the congregation are English teaching from other countries -- like Canada, the US, New Zealand and the UK. They have come to Korea to teach English at special schools called "Hagwons" where parents will send their children each day after their regular school, so that they can get additional instruction in English-language skills. I spoke to a young Korean boy "John" who was 12 and he told me about his school and his hagwon also. Sounds a little like "Hogwarts" so I said to him that he was going to a school like Harry Potter and he smiled.

Every one at Joyful Church has invited me to come back and visit with them again, but they want me to bring my wife along next time. I said we would be glad to come if the Lord opens those doors in the future. Now, I need to pack and then get to bed by no later than 10pm tonight. My alarm will be set for 4am. The taxi is due to pick me up by 5:15am to drive me to the Pohang airport. Once I get over to Gimpo, I will need to take the bus to Incheon. My departure on Korean Air is scheduled for noon and it is to arrive into Chicago-O'Hare Airport around 11am Monday. I have a couple of hours -- to get through customs and everything, and then I'll catch my final connection down home to St. Louis-Lambert about 2:45 pm or so. I'm due to arrive back in St. Louis right about 4pm or a little thereafter.

3

A Few More Steps along the Way

After returning to my teaching position in the United States in the fall term of 2004, I continued to stay in contact with colleagues at Handong. In January, 2005, and again in January, 2008, I joined Prof. S.K. Lee and Handong students on projects in Thailand and Cambodia. Then in the summer of 2009, I was invited to apply for a visiting professorship at Handong in the undergraduate U.S. & International Law program.

July 11, 2009

I have now completed the application documents requested by Handong for the faculty position they have invited me to accept for this coming academic year -- teaching American law in their undergraduate international law program of study. All of my teaching will be in English, though I'm hoping to improve my Korean beyond my current knowledge which consists only of "kamsahamnida" which means "thank you." I have also just booked my one-way flight to Busan, departing August 20. One of my new colleagues from Handong is scheduled to meet me upon arrival and then accompany me on the two-hour drive north to Pohang and Handong's campus. I will hit the ground running since the fall faculty retreat is set to commence on August 24 with class instruction beginning September 1.

July 17, 2009

Continued Planning & Preparations

This past evening, I had the privilege of participating in an international telephone conference call with two esteemed members of the School of Law faculty at Handong. Prof. Ji and Prof. Kim posed engaging questions on the topics of the relationship between faith and law and the substantive areas of law I will be teaching in the School of Law's UIL (United States & International Law) major field of study. As I take yet a few more steps along this path, I continue to sense a confirming peace in my heart and mind that encourages me to keep depending upon God's grace and pursuing His will. I greatly value your on-going prayers. I would especially appreciate your praying Psalm 121.

July 23, 2009

A Conversation with Korea via Skype

By most accounts, Korea, along with the rest of East Asia, is considered a generation or so ahead of the U.S. in its technology. Everyone is connected. When you spot a friend across the street, the best way to get his attention is not to shout out, but rather to call him on his mobile. So, when I was asked to prepare for a web cam interview with Handong's Academic Affairs Committee, I anticipated that any technological deficiencies would be on my end of the Internet; not the other way around.

As I sat in front of my newly installed web cam at 11pm last night, though, it soon became evident that the versions of MSN Messenger, which my soon-to-be colleagues at Handong and I were attempting to use for the video call, were not communicating with one another. We could see each other with remarkable clarity, but alas, we had no audio connection. I suggested, by way of an instant text message, that we each download Skype and re-attempt our video call. To my surprise, my Korean colleague was not familiar with Skype, but in a mere matter of minutes, he had downloaded and installed the service.

Soon thereafter, my live video interview with three professors comprising the Academic Affairs Committee, commenced, and we enjoyed a delightful "face-to-face" conversation. I recounted my first meeting with Associate Dean Hee Eun Lee of Handong International Law School (HILS) along with Prof. Kuyper Lee at a conference in Washington, DC, in the fall of 2003. That meeting, in turn, led to my visiting professorship at HILS in the summer of 2004. The Committee members were also pleased to hear of my work with Prof. Sang Ki Lee and Handong students in Cambodia during my missions there in January of 2005 and again in 2008.

In addition to recounting my previous cross-cultural experiences abroad, I also shared briefly about my participating in the International MBA program at Fontbonne University where I've had the opportunity to teach students from Taiwan, Thailand, China, and Cambodia, as well as Korea, over the past four years. In ways that I would never have imagined no less than ten years ago, the Lord has been forming and preparing me for further service to the people of East Asia -- including, even now, introducing at least a few to the technological benefits of Skype.

July 30, 2009

Finishing another Fontbonne Term

This past week, I had the great pleasure of attending the graduation ceremony for the 2009 International MBA class at Fontbonne University. Seven of my students were from Taipei, Taiwan. Its an intensive 12-month program of study. The students take four courses each term. My class -- Business Ethics -- was one of the four in their final term. Since Fontbonne is a Catholic university, there is a strong emphasis on forming strong ethical character across the entire curriculum. Beyond merely discussing ethical theories, I address the role of personal faith as a foundation for ethical practice and the need we all have for on-going self-examination. It has been a blessing to be a part of the International program for the past four years. My experiences with these students (nearly all of whom are East Asian) have nurtured my sense of calling to Asia and now, to Korea once again.

I'm 22 days away from my currently scheduled departure date. I will be submitting my application for a university teaching visa with the Korean consulate in Chicago within the next several days. Once the visa is in hand, I only need to complete packing my bags for the journey and preparing to ship my books on ahead so they will arrive in time for my class preparations. The fall term at Handong begins 1 Sep.

July 31, 2009

A Telephone Call from the President

The President of Handong Global University, that is -- I've just concluded a delightfully cordial telephone conversation with President Young Gil Kim. I first met President Kim in the summer of 2004 when I was serving as a visiting professor at Handong International Law School. He fondly recalled that meeting in his office on the campus of Handong where I was introduced to him by my mentor, Prof. SK Lee. I learned that President Kim has a Missouri connection. He earned his M.S. in metallurgical engineering at the University of Missouri - Rolla in 1967. He then went on to earn his Ph.D. in materials science and engineering at the Rensselaer Polytechnic Institute in New York. President Kim has led Handong to become well-known as a university with a global vision that seeks to educate servant leaders who are responsible agents for change in the world that brings glory to God. I was deeply encouraged by his words and the warm greeting he extended to me as I will be shortly joining the faculty at Handong.

August 20, 2009

Final Pieces Being Put in Place

Some folks might say "the pieces are falling into place," but as I have experienced life over these past two weeks, it is quite clear to me that each of the necessary pieces to complete my preparation for departure have been artfully put in their place by His hand. Last Thursday, I hauled nine boxes of my law & theology books up to the shipping company's depot near the airport. On the advice of one of the office clerks and with the assistance of the owner's son, I placed all of the books in plastic bags and re-packed them for their sea-going voyage. Although I was frustrated by the need to repack the books, the extra time on the shipping dock gave me the opportunity to speak with Brandon. He had studied philosophy and ethics at university, so the conversation took us into considering questions like how to best live life in our contemporary world.

Over the weekend, Sandy and I enjoyed a wonderfully refreshing time on retreat in the Arkansas Ozark's at the Little Portion Retreat Center outside of Eureka Springs. Michael Card led the retreat on the theme "Hesed: A Portrait of God." Hesed is the Hebrew word that is often translated "loving-kindness" or "mercy" as in "Let us give thanks to the Lord, for His mercy endures forever." (Psalm 136) Not only did we experience an abundance of blessings from God's hand through Michael's teachings on hesed, we also had the pleasure of unexpectedly seeing friends from my time serving with the Christian Legal Society.

Unbeknown to us, Sam and Jill Casey as well as Dave and Jean

Allen had planned to attend the very same retreat. Sam is now General Counsel for Advocates International, an organization of Christian attorneys from over 100 countries. I also learned that Sam is planning to come to Handong in June 2010 to teach a course on Jurisprudence. God has gracious ways of confirming His direction in our lives!

Finally, upon our return to St. Louis, I found that my E-1 visa had been delivered to our house via Fed Ex from the Korean Consulate in Chicago. I also received my residency certification from the IRS. These were the two remaining key documents I needed to have in hand before I could depart; so now I'm fully documented and readied for travel. Today, I spent packing my bags and enjoying the fellowship of my family at a bar-b-que hosted by my daughter and son-in-law. I was even enabled to see my grand daughter Taya off on the school bus that took her to her first day of kindergarten. Tomorrow morning -- final packing with departure set for the evening hours.

All in all, I've sensed God's good hand as He has been graciously and mercifully watching over "my going out . . . from this day forward" (Psalm 121) even as the journey continues . . .

First Year

4

Reminders along the Journey

August 24, 2009

By God's good and gracious hand, I have arrived safe and sound here at Handong. Each stage along my flight travel path was marked with reminders of God's presence. My connections from St. Louis to Los Angeles (LAX) and then along to Seoul (INC) Incheon were smooth sailing and on time. I even was able to sleep a total of 6 hours on the 12 hour flight across the Pacific – well actually, the flight path went north to Alaska and the over the Bering Strait to the eastern coast of Russia and down ultimately to Korea. There was hardly any turbulence and the flight seemed like the shortest I've ever flown from the U.S. to Asia.

Once I arrived at Incheon International Airport (one of the largest in the world and recently rated one of the best) very early Saturday morning (Korean time), I began to encounter those reminders I mentioned before. As I made my way through Immigration and Customs, I was directed toward an elevator that would convey me from the International terminal to the Domestic one, though, I wasn't sure which way I was to go upon leaving the elevator. I was provided a guide in the person of Kim Jong Il (not the dear leader of the North but a pastor of a Presbyterian Church in the city of Daegu).

As we conversed during the elevator ride he asked me where I was headed, and I said that I was looking for the Asiana flight over to Busan and then from there I would be provided a ride up to Pohang where I would be teaching at Handong Global University. To my very pleasant surprise, Pastor Kim advised me that he not along knew of Handong, he had even met Prof. S.K. Lee while on a mission trip last year in Phnom Penh, Cambodia. This was an amazing and wonderful confirmation of the Lord's direction.

While back in St. Louis, it was not usual for me to experience two degrees of separation when I met a person for the first time (the person knew someone that I also knew – since as it is often said, that St. Louis is the biggest small town in America), but to experience two degrees of separation with the very first person I met in Korea was simply a wonder! As we continued to talk, Pastor Kim told me that he was also familiar with Covenant Seminary in St. Louis since he too was a Presbyterian. He had even heard President Bryan Chapel from Covenant preach at a sister seminary in Seoul a few years back. In short course, Pastor Kim had guided me to the Asiana ticket counter, encouraged me in the Lord, and even invited me to preach at his church in Daegu which is only an hour's drive from Pohang. Any yet, the reminders of God's presence and directing hand were only beginning.

As I sat down near the ticket counter, I noticed a sign indicating that the counter would not be open for over an hour. No problem, I had plenty of time to check-in and make my connecting flight to Busan later that morning, so I settled in a chair nearby and began to read. I soon noticed a young lady at the end of my row who also had an open Bible in her lap that she was reading in between times of closing her eyes and opening her palms upward it what I could only conclude was a posture of prayer. How often would you see that in an American airport? It was to me another gracious reminder of God's presence in this amazing country!

Later, when I took my place in the ticket line, I was standing just behind a young Korean woman who turned to ask me, in nearly perfect English, where I was traveling. When I said that my final destination was Handong University in Pohang, a smile came over her face. She told me that she was on her way home to Busan from California (she had actually been on the very same flight I was on from Los Angeles to Seoul). She had just graduated from a small college in California where her aunt and uncle lived. Before college, she had also attended a Christian high school in Lancaster, Pennsylvania – totaling six years in the States and explaining why her English was so fluent.

Her smile, though, came from the fact that she was in the process of applying to attend Handong in the next academic year. I don't know who was more encouraged by the encounter – her or me. The young lady's name was Ms. Choi and she said that while she was very excited about the opportunity to attend Handong, she was a bit apprehensive because she did not know if she could meet the university's rigorous admission standards. I encouraged her to seek God's calling on her life and trust Him to lead and open the doors for her further education and service.

A few moments later, Ms. Choi struck up a conversation with a young, blond, mid-20ish looking American fellow standing behind me. He was on his way back to a town in the country side of Korea where he will be starting his second year as an English teacher. I was shortly brought into the conversation and learned that the young man had graduated from Colorado Christian University in Denver. He is also planning hoping to do graduate studies in international relations after he finishes his second of teaching.

I commended him for choosing a great "gap year" experience (though in his case, it was "gap years" – the year or two between completing one's undergraduate studies and before going on to graduate or professional school) and then told him of my son Caleb and daughter-in-law Micaela's experiences traveling around the world with Willing Workers on Organic Farms. Now, this young man now began to smile. His name was Caleb, too! While many might say this was just another "coincidence," in my book of life experiences, it was yet again a small, yet wonderful reminder of God's presence and guidance in our paths. And, those reminders were still to continue this day.

Upon my arrival in Busan, I was met by the smiling face of Professor Seong Hoon Kim, who directs the undergraduate international law program in which I will be teaching as a visiting professor this year. During a beautiful two-hour drive north along the eastern coast of Korea, I learned that Prof. Kim and I shared a number of professional experiences. He too had practiced for a large law firm before leaving the practice to teach. One of his main practice areas was, like mine, business litigation. His area of special interest in his teaching focuses on Antitrust and other unfair competition laws. The course I had taught at Handong International Law School back in the summer of 2004 was U.S. Antitrust law.

And the parallels don't end there. Not only is Prof. Kim engaged in full-time teaching at the University, he is also a PhD candidate at a university in Seoul where he travels each week to attend one class a term. For the past three years while teaching at Fontbonne, I've been a PhD student at Concordia Seminary, taking one class a term. And, while his studies concentrate on Korean business competition law and my studies revolve around the intersection of law and theology via ethics, we both need to gain a competency in the German language – for him, because German law has been the greatest influence upon the development of Korean business (commercial) law and for me, so that I can read Bonhoeffer in his the language in which he wrote.

Are you saying "coincidence" again? Well, maybe – but when so many are added one upon another in such a short space of time, I can only say that they have been an amazing series of touches to my heart and mind as I undertake this new beginning in a place half-way around the world from those I hold so dear who I've been called, at least for a time, to leave behind. And, you might say that the reminders I've experienced thus far in this day should be more than enough to encourage any doubting heart, but God was not finished reminding me that he not only was now directing my path but that He has also been directing it to this place at this time for many months and years past.

This final reminder came after Prof. Kim had treated me to a great Korean bar-b-que lunch and then shown me to my apartment in the University's faculty guesthouse. As I was settling-in to the apartment, I noticed that there were a few items I needed from the campus convenience store. So, I took the short walk to the store and began searching for the items I needed. I walked up and down several aisles and then turned to the next only to nearly collide with a young man – a student – in fact, a law student from Phnom Penh, Cambodia. I had met Samnang there in January, 2008, when I was with Prof. S.K. Lee teaching a seminar to both Cambodian and Korean law students at the Royal University of Law & Economics. Sam is the first of the RULE students to come to study at Handong International Law School. His smile was the biggest of all that had greeted me this day!

My first day here at Handong came to a delightful conclusion as Prof. Eric Enlow (also from St. Louis) and his young son, Gunner, came over to my apartment with their arms full of treats and household items – a warmer welcome wagon gift has never been given! We enjoyed an encouraging conversation as I recounted to Eric how God has been extending His gracious hand of blessing through reminders of His presence throughout the past 24 hours. The verse from Psalms came often to mind: Let us give thanks unto the Lord for He is good, and His mercy is everlasting!

August 25, 2009

An Alien Experience

Have you ever felt like an alien? Are you an alien? For the first time in my life I both feel like an alien and I am one, too. Well, that's what the folks at the local Korean Immigration Office call me. I was taken there today in order to apply for my "Alien Registration Card." In Korea, if you're an alien, it is, without question, the card that you don't leave home without -- move over American Express! My experience being an alien, though, provided me yet another opportunity to meet and get to know a new colleague, Prof. B. Harry Jee.

Though a native of Korea, Prof. Jee has been in the States for many years and is a U.S. Citizen. So like me, he had to come to the Immigration Office and obtain an alien registration card. It looks a lot like a driver's license, but it opens so many more doors in this highly regulated land. Without it, you can't open a bank account or even go to see a doctor -- but with it, all the benefits of living in Korea are afforded you -- well nearly. Prof. Jee explained that Korea, though a democracy (technically), is a closely regulated and guarded country. All of the various governmental agencies share information about citizens and registered aliens alike.

Prof. Jee teaches management, finance and business ethics. Before starting his academic career at Penn State and then serving as Dean of the School of Business at The King's College in New York City for the past six years, Harry had worked for both J.P. Morgan and an international investment banking firm based in Seoul and New York. He was quite the jet-setter, sometimes even traveling around the world in a week as he transacted business in Seoul, New York and London along the way. While waiting in line at the local bank, we shared experiences from our professional lives and realized that both of us had encountered similar challenges as Christians in the throws of the business and legal arenas. Harry's deep concern for imparting a strong sense and practice of business ethics to his students grows out of his own admitted failures to stay true to the path of integrity in the midst of heavy pressures in the business world.

What an encouragement to meet a brother in Christ who is so authentic and genuine! It is exciting for me to realize that I will be benefiting from the devotedness of Prof. Jee as well as his outstanding academic background and professional experiences. Harry truly embodies the spirit and vision of Handong University and, by God's grace and mercy, I hope to be formed and shaped by my service here into a more devoted and responsible follower of Christ in the midst of the concrete realities of life in the here and now -- even though I be an alien in this new land.

August 26, 2009

Happy Anniversary, My Love!

Today marks the 31st anniversary of my marriage to Sandy. It is the first anniversary, however, in those 31 years that we have spent apart -- by the distance of half-way around the globe. The most difficult challenge I had to face in responding to the call to teach here at Handong was the reality that the first few months would be a time of separation from the one person whom God designed to complete me and counter-balance me in every dimension of my life.

When God calls us, though, He grants sustaining grace and the encouragement and support of both family and fellow members of the Body of Christ. He also has given us many great memories and experiences along our path walking together. A little more than a year ago, Sandy and I were celebrating our 30th anniversary near the top of Haleakala just as morning was dawning on the Island of Maui. My mother had given us a wonderful gift of a week's stay on the island. Shortly after dawn that morning, we hopped on touring bikes and road down that volcanic mountain as we enjoyed the amazing views of the island and the Pacific! It was without a doubt the highlight of our stay on Maui.

The Lord also gives sustaining grace through the wonders of technology. Both my laptop here and our home pc back in Fenton are equipped with webcams, so Sandy and I have been able to video call one another via Skype. Just being able to see her face in real time and hear her voice is a true source of joy. Thank you so much, Honey, for an amazing journey together over these 31 years! I'm so looking forward to the coming months when you will be joining me here. Until then, hold me in your heart.

August 27, 2009

Consider the Birds of the Air . . .

No matter where in the world you may be, God displays the wonders of His creation. While he walked the earth, Jesus would often refer to aspects of creation as a means of deepening our understanding of the Father's love and care for His own. One of my favorite commands of Christ is: "Look at the birds of the air" (Matthew 6:26) During my first week here at Handong, I've had the opportunity to take several morning and evening walks. Along the way, I've been treated to a wonderful display of the beauty of God's creation through the birds of Asia.

A purple heron was flying low over the rice fields in the valley behind the Mission House where my apartment is located. Then, while on my morning walk today, I spotted a little guy who I thought was related to a gold finch, but now I think she was most likely a mountain fulvetta. During my second lap around the campus, I heard a strange call in the trees that lined the south side of the road along the edge of campus near the Student Center.

Using my "ears as eyes," I followed the sound of the call until I came upon a very large bird perched about 10 feet up in a tree. It looked like a magpie, but its coloring was more black and light blue, rather than black with patches of white.

When I searched through the gallery of Asian Bird photo's, I found that he is called an Asian Fairy Bluebird -- amazing! One of the biggest bluebirds I've ever seen. He's about 3x's the size of an Eastern Bluebird! As I was just about to end my walk and return to the apartment some movement caught my eye in the rice fields that extend to the southeast side of campus. When I stopped to check it out, I was delighted to see again a Great Egret -- elder cousin of the Snowy White that inhabits the river bottoms along the Meramec and Missouri. These are just of few of the wonders of God's creation that have joined together to greet me in this wondrous land! Even the little sparrow I spotted brought to mind Christ's promise that not even one sparrow can fall to the ground without the Father's knowledge! What a caring and encouraging God we serve!

August 28, 2009

Foxes have Holes and Birds of the Air have Their Nests, but . . . .

When a disciple responds to the call to follow, it is not a given that he will always be provided a "place to lay his head." At a minimum, it would be inappropriate for the follower to complain about his living accommodations. So, I was thankful when told that I would have a "studio apartment" in the Mission House on the south side of campus. Though smaller than a typical room at your local Motel 6, it provides more than adequate space for all the bare necessities of life. I have a bed and desk, table and chairs, small couch, TV (English channels are CNN & the BBC) and a fully-equipped Asian kitchenette.

The combination "toilet, shower & sink" bathroom is around the corner from the kitchenette, just to the right when coming in the front door. That's right!! The whole room is the shower. Though my apartment (room) is somewhat Spartan, I was quite overwhelmed when I was shown into my faculty office in the new All Nations Hall. The office itself entails more square footage than my apartment! So far, the support staff has moved in a desk, credenza, conference table and chairs, file cabinets, fan (the in-room air conditioning is not yet operational) and one of two bookcases. This afternoon, my computer was installed and connected to the University network. I even have dial tone on my phone! Below you'll see a view looking into my office from the hallway. My nine boxes of books are still en route by ship sailing over the Pacific and are not due to arrive for several more weeks. As a result my bookcases will be a bit bare until then.

All in all, I'm very thankful for the provisions made for me here. The office is undoubtedly the largest I've ever had, even when I compare it to the one's I worked in during my years at Lewis Rice. The apartment will do me good during these first few months. When Sandy and I return after the first of the year, we'll be moved into the family apartments on the north side of campus.

August 30, 2009

Welcomed into a Worshipping Community

This morning, I was warmly welcomed -- along with other new faculty and students -- into the worshipping community of Handong International Church or "HIC" -- (I'm finding that the folks here really like using acronyms). I thought this was quite appropriate for a feller from Fenton -- I fit in well with the HIC's. (My apologies to my family, friends and neighbors in Fenton).

The service is conducted entirely in English. We sang worship songs that are well-known among American evangelical churches, like "Your Name is a Strong and Mighty Tower" and "Blessed Be the Name of the Lord." Following the time of singing, the worship leader invited the congregation to gather around those of us -- students and faculty, alike -- who were new to the fellowship (He had asked us to stand). The members of the congregation then prayed for God's blessing upon our time of teaching and learning at Handong. It was a very warm and heart-felt expression of love and welcome!

Pastor Young preached a message from 1 Samuel 2 on the life of Eli. It was an insightful and challenging sermon that called upon us all to examine ourselves and to see whether we are just living outwardly religious lives -- like Eli -- but with the hears of our soul dull to the transformative power of the Word of God. He spoke from his heart and called upon the congregation to pray for God's mercy. Since Eli's only hope was in the God's promise that "I will raise up for myself a faithful priest, who shall do according to what is in my heart and in my mind." (1 Samuel 2:35), so also our only hope is in God Himself -- the Lord Jesus. He alone has the ability to save us and enable us to live authentic lives even though we are sinners, because He in His mercy forgives and grant us a new heart and renews our spirit in Him!

Following the service, I had the opportunity to meet and begin to get to know several more students from the States -- many from Le Tourneau University in Longview, Texas -- as well as new colleagues on the undergraduate faculty. I was also encouraged to see and visit briefly again with Prof. Harry Jee who I had met this past week on the trip to the Immigration Office. This evening, the church has invited all the new students and faculty to a fellowship dinner. Assistant Pastor Dave Becket encouraged everyone to come and called for a show of hands so that they will be sure to have plenty of food. Evidently, eating together is a regular practice of this local church. I thought for sure I would be losing some weight during my first few months living alone here, but now, I'm beginning to think I -- like the ravens -- will be well supplied by my heavenly Father.

August 31, 2009

After Months of Prep - My First Day of Teaching

The day has finally arrived! My first class at Handong is U.S. Business Law & Management. Thirty-two students (make that 33, when a young man decided to register today) -- from all regions of Korea, yes -- but also from Mongolia, Afghanistan, Tajikistan, South Africa, England, Haiti and even -- would you believe -- Minnesota! It is truly amazing to be given the opportunity to teach such a diverse group of students -- to be apart of the world community!

Today's class didn't begin until 4:45pm, so I had the entire day to work in my office; preparing my course syllabus, lecture notes and outline. And even though I have been working on my class preparation for over a week, I still managed to make a mathematical error in calculating the total points from the case studies, unit exams and final examination that I've planned for the course. It's good, though, to admit such a basic mistake the first day to demonstrate that I'm just a regular guy -- or at least that's what I tell myself.

Another wondrous thing about teaching here at Handong is the fact that the university encourages the faculty to not only think about the impact of our Christian faith on the subjects we teach, but also to practice our faith before our students. So, I explained to the class that it would be my practice to begin each session with a prayer since in praying we acknowledge that God exists and we admit that we need Him. And then, we prayed together and sought God's blessing and direction in our learning.

After covering the course syllabus and an overview of the class topics, I concluded the class with a brief account of my own law school experiences. I had written about them some years ago, and I thought it might be a good way to introduce myself to my fellow law students. Here's what I read to them:

The Three Longest Years

In the summer of 1983, I was looking ahead to three years of law school. If what I had read in Scott Turow's book One L, and what I had seen portrayed by John Houseman in the film The Paper Chase, was right, I was on the threshold of three of the most difficult and challenging years – the three longest years – of my life. I had come to law school at Saint Louis University married and with three small children, yet still convinced that I was heeding God's call. Succeeding was not my first concern; survival would be sufficient. I found assurance in the story of Daniel and his companions who were forced by their captors to study for three years in Babylon, but were preserved by God and through his strength stood firm in faith. (Daniel 1)

The first year started well enough. My journal entries for those early months in the fall of '83 contain scattered references to "opportunities to speak to others about the things of God," "speaking at length to a 3d year student who is a Mormon" and even a few brief accounts of Bible studies with fellow law students. But, by the middle of the spring term, the journal read "preoccupied with school work and job projects . . . so no regular personal quiet time." Though I had begun my studies as a believer seeking to practice the discipline of daily devotions, the demands of law school had steadily pushed Bible reading and prayer time out of my daily routine. I started thinking less about God and more about me.

I had succumbed to the first year of law school. It had indeed "scared me to death," and as I entered the second year, I was well on my way to being "worked to death." My journal attests to this since I had completely left-off all entries by the summer of '84. Although I had been convinced that the Lord was leading me to law school, I was no longer looking to Him to lead me through it. I began pursuing my own personal interests rather than seeking my family's best interests. When interviews came around for summer internships, I signed-up with the big firms in hopes of landing a select position. Clerking for one of the largest firms in St. Louis that summer, I was lured all the more into aspiring to a life of affluence. Unlike my hero Daniel in Babylon, I began to dine at the king's table.

My third year experience was true to form. I was, for the most part, "bored to death." I had a prize offer to join the firm with whom I had done my internship. They even agreed to fore go the ordinary rotation through their other practice areas and allowed me to plan on moving right into litigation. I was set. What I had forgotten, though, was how I had come to succeed when at first my thought had only been of survival. I was reminded through failure. I failed to win the trial advocacy competition and I failed to attain the final class rank for which I had been striving. Through those failures, the Lord called me back to him and gave me a renewed sense of his grace and of my need for constant dependence upon him. He alone had given me the grace and knowledge to succeed through my three longest years.

To these four young men God gave knowledge and understanding of all kinds of literature and learning. ~ Daniel 1:17

After class, several students stayed behind and expressed their appreciation. Two even wanted to work as my teaching assistant. On the whole, though, this first day of class has been a challenge.

I'm truly exhausted, physically (from all the walking across campus and climbing of stairs -- did I tell you that my class is in a different building than my office?) as well as emotionally. I would greatly value your continued prayers for God's grace and strength through each day.

5

September 1, 2009

"Hop-along" -- my new Korean name

I'm walking with a bit of limp these past few days. At first, I thought it might be a shin splint. I'm doing an awful lot of walking -- more than I'm used to, I think. I do enjoy walking, but all I'm doing these days is walking and climbing steps -- lots of them. So, I've been experiencing this throbbing pain in the lower part of my left leg. I've also been experiencing a bit of swelling in the area. I have been icing it up each evening and elevating it, but the pain is still persisting. This makes the fourth day. I've also started to wear my tennis shoes all the time, thinking that my hard-soled shoes (even though they are Ecco's) may also be contributing to the pain production.

Now, one of my colleagues has suggested that I may have developed a thrombosis. So, I'm taking some extra aspirin (per Sandy's recommendation in her most recent email to me) and I'll be going to see the doctor tomorrow morning -- I'm due to have the regular medical exam that all new international faculty are given in any case, so I'm hoping the doctor will be able to diagnose my pain's origin and provide the needed treatment. It's good to walk with a limp, though. Jacob did after that late night wrestling match of his. And, I think Paul may have even walked with sort of a limp (whatever that "thorn in the flesh" might have been). So, when we have a limp, we're in good company. Limps remind us that we are always in need of support beyond ourselves -- that we need the grace of Christ for each step. I was reminded of this foundational truth in one of my recent quite time readings: *We have this treasure in jars of clay, to show that the surpassing power belongs to God and not to us.* ~ 2 Corinthians 4:7 At our best, we are but jars of clay. And in most cases, those jars are marred by cracks. He alone restores and equips us for His purpose in each day! By grace we are saved! So, go ahead, just call me "Hopalong" -- I think it may become my new Korean name.

September 2, 2009

Now I'm officially an Alien

Well, there it is. I'm officially a documented and registered alien here in the Republic of Korea. After several of us new faculty picked up our registration cards at the Immigration Office, we were then driven by Ms. Iris Kim, from the University's International Affairs Office, to Good Samaritan Hospital where we all underwent the routine medical exam which we were told would only take 20 minutes -- that's 20 minutes for each of the six of us -- so we ended up spending the next two hours walking about the hospital from department to department -- blood pressure, EKG, eye exam, hearing exam, dental exam, chest X-ray, blood and urine tests.

They are very thorough. They even checked my blood pressure three times since on the first two attempts my reading was a bit on the high side -- 157/82 at first. The nurse thought I might have had too big of a breakfast (I'd made myself two eggs fried, bacon and toast -- a good Western breakfast, right?) On the third try, I was down in the 120's/80's range. The nurse looked at me and said, "OK, you pass." After completing our medical exams, we had planned to go by the local bank and open account, but several of my colleagues had to get back for departmental meetings. Those of us who need to do our banking will be heading back to town tomorrow morning. On the whole, it was a nice little outing. Prof. Harry Jee was along again, and three new English language faculty from Canada -- a couple, George and Nancy, and Debi van Duin, all from Winnipeg.

This morning at our first faculty chapel, I was warmly greeted by a dear older sister, Gayle Henrotte, from San Francisco. She is such an encouraging soul -- she could be Helen Horn's twin sister! Pastor Young Hwang preached a challenging message from James 1:5-8 and reminded us that wisdom comes only from God, not through the intellectual capabilities of humans. Handong is a place of learning, yes, but even more important is gaining the wisdom of God for living responsibly in the here and now! The service concluded with an extended time of intercessory prayer and the hearty singing of "More Love For Thee." What a way to start a day! Each day I'm encouraged by the vitality of life here. I'm experiencing in deeper ways the reality of life together under the Word.

September 3, 2009

Meet Mr. Mok

Earlier this week, I was pleasantly surprised to learn that each professor on the faculty of the School of Law at Handong is entitled to hire a teaching assistant (a "TA" -- remember the fondness for acronyms!). So, I was encouraged by the law school staff to announce to my students that I would be taking applications for a TA. I did, and within moments after my very first class, two eager students approached me and expressed their interest in the job.

I interviewed both a day later and, again to my surprise, found that one of my applicants had both excellent English language skills and experience as a TA for one of the other professors on the law school faculty -- he already knew all of the ropes! Little did I suspect, though, that the scope of duties for a TA here at Handong included not only assistance in making copies of handouts for class and grading papers (like a typical TA in the States) but also helping me arrange and decorate my office, making my morning tea, going shopping for me, providing me a ride into town when needed, helping me obtain a mobile phone, and at the end of every day, even cleaning my office!

I had been told by my good friend Dr. John Han that I would be treated like royalty here, but I never imagined that it would entail having my own personal assistant, chauffeur and butler all rolled into one! But that just what my TA is. So, let me introduce to you, Mr. Younghoon Mok. He is a senior here at Handong majoring in both U.S. & International Law (UIL) and International Relations. He studied for six years in New York and Maryland where he went to Middle School and High School graduating from St. Paul's in Brooklandville, Maryland in 2002. (Interestingly, I graduated from St. Paul's [no relation, though] in Concordia, Missouri -- but that was in 1977).

Mr. Mok's English skills are outstanding! He's an absolute whiz on the computer, and he's already started to decorate my office with a nice little plant! The other law school professors have stopped by to say what a good choice I've made. They all know Younghoon as both an excellent student in the UIL program and as an exceptional TA who served one of the senior members of the faculty this past year. I see him as just another one of God's gracious provisions for me here. I am continually amazed by the ways that God encourages us as we seek, by His grace alone, to serve His purpose in this our generation.

I know without a doubt that I've never yet been in a teaching post where I have been so encouraged and supported as I am here teaching at Handong. Its truly wonderful to be enabled to do what you believe you have been designed and equipped by God's call to do -- to serve others according to His will and purpose, day-by-day, step-by-step.

September 5, 2009

Korean Hospitality

Somehow I always had the idea that Southern hospitality was the hallmark for all who seek to welcome "strangers and sojourners" along the ways of life -- you know, Hebrews 13:2-styled hospitality. But after two weeks in here at Handong, I think the new standard is Korean! Not only was I treated to a delightful luncheon at a seaside Chinese restaurant this past Thursday with my colleagues from the School of Law, I was also invited, along with the other new international faculty to a lavish five-course dinner Friday evening. The dinner was hosted by the staff of the Handong International Church: Pastor Young Hwang (who is also a theology professor at the University) and his wife Min, Pastor Dave Becket and his wife Kim (who is a first year law student at HILS). The group also included Prof. Harry Jee, my new friend from King's College in NYC; Pat & Kathy Talbot (Pat is a professor at HILS), Debi van Duin, new faculty in the Department of Language Education (DLE) and Dr. Wilhelm Holzafel. He's from Germany by way of South Africa and has been teaching life sciences at Handong for 2 1/2 years. Wilhelm is a wonderful brother who I asked to tutor me in German while I'm here, so that I can make some progress on my PhD studies and maybe even be able to read Bonhoeffer in the language in which he wrote before the year is out! We'll see. Before the evening's conversations were concluded, Pastor Hwang had asked to consider teaching some theology classes next semester.

September 6, 2009

A Global Community

When I had taught here at Handong back in 2004, I met only the Korean and American faculty of the International Law School (HILS). I am beginning to realize now, however, that I have not only been welcomed into a cross-national relationship (Korean-American), but I'm also becoming a part of a truly global community. This came home to me Sunday morning after church in a particularly personal way -- through the fellowship extended to me by my new colleague Prof. Wilhelm Holzapfel from Germany. Wilhelm gathered a group of students and faculty alike and treated us to a Kaffeeklatsch at his apartment on campus. Our small group reflected the wondrous diversity of this truly global university! We represented three continents and a variety of religious traditions. Our conversation ranged from sharing summer travel experiences to pondering theological paradoxes.

It was a delightful time! I think I may have even persuaded Wilhelm to consider becoming my German tutor so that I can pursue my language studies here and be prepared to sit for my German translation examination when I return to my study at Concordia Seminary this coming year. Who would have thought that I could come to Korea and study German while teaching American Law? On my walk back across campus following our Kaffeeklatsch, my global experiences expanded to the Land Down Under as I met and exchanged "Good'aye, mate!" with Alex Banks, an Aussie from Queensland. Later, I met a student from Congo. That makes five continents, now! The world is growing smaller and I hope we are all growing closer as brothers and sisters.

September 7, 2009

Re-Learning Some of the Basic Lessons of Life

I have been told that nearly every international faculty member who comes to Handong makes a trip to the local hospital's Emergency Room within about the first two months of their sojourn. Well, it seems I have been given that privilege in my first two weeks! Here's how it transpired.

It all started -- as every life-instructing experience does -- in a very ordinary way. I was fixing myself a light Sunday evening supper and needed to remove a bottle cap. I reached in the kitchenette drawer of my well-anointed, little studio apartment. In that drawer, I found nearly every utensil you might need for meal preparation -- except -- a bottle-cap opener. So being the resourceful Eagle Scout that I am (this will come back to haunt me), I picked up a small knife and started to pry off, ever so carefully, that stubborn bottle cap.

I thought if I could only loosen the edges of the cap, I could then twist it off. What I failed to do, however, was what my father had regularly warned me to always do when using a knife or tool. Think about what might happen if the knife slips! Seems as though at fifty I was in need of re-learning this most basic of life's lessons: Consider carefully the consequences of your actions.

That's right; you guessed it. The cap popped-off a whole lot easier than I had expected and -- yes -- the knife slipped. But the other thing I had failed to check was just how sharp this little knife was. It had a rounded blade, so I assumed it was more like a dinner knife -- not a razor-sharp pairing knife. In a moment, in a twinkling of an eye, my left index finger was changed! Laid open with a inch-long slice that was clearly too deep just to bind-up tightly and butterfly closed. No, I was no longer in need of Korean hospitality -

- this would require professional medical attention. Thankfully, Eric Enlow and his family had just dropped me off back at my apartment (The Hermitage, as I have now affectionately come to call it) an hour before, so after wrapping a clean hand towel around my wound and applying direct pressure (remember I'm an Eagle Scout), I made a quick call to Eric and humbly requested his prompt assistance. He assured me he would be right over to pick me up and drive me into Pohang's Good Samaritan Hospital.

What my good brother did not tell me at the time was that he was in the middle of grilling up his family's dinner. He dropped everything to come to my aid. We made it to the hospital in less than 30 minutes, and though I don't think I had loss much blood, I was feeling a bit light-headed. Eric directed me around from the main entrance to the ER -- having four kids, as Eric does, he has come to know this route fairly well. In fact (remember the two-month rule?), his young son (about 6 at the time) broke his leg within their first few months at Handong. After being given two shots -- one in the arm, an antibiotic, the other in my rump for tetanus -- and two X-rays of my hand, the attending physician came over to my gurney and attended to the wound. It wasn't hurting much by this time since I had continued to apply pressure, but being the careful doc that he was, he needed to open the wound up and clean it out thoroughly.

Now the pain really intensified, but I was put in my place by the fellow two gurneys down from me. He had just been brought into the ER with a compound fracture of his lower leg! So it was time for me to buck-up and take the pain that clearly paled in light of his suffering. Six artfully crafted stitches drew the 3cm wound tightly closed. The finger was bandaged and I was sent off with a 3-day prescription of antibiotics and pain medication. The whole experience had taken a little less than 2 hours and the cost -- $101.46 (that's 125,590 Won) which included the X-rays, medications and stitches! Consider that on your way to health care reform in the States. So now, I'm walking around campus and soon to conduct my Monday afternoon class with a fairly large bandage on my left index finger. My "learning opportunity" has been especially humbling when you consider that about 35 years ago, this Eagle Scout nearly cut off that very same finger with an ax when he was attempting to spilt some oak logs on the first evening of his last Summer Camp as Senior Patrol Leader of his troop. Not only was it the same finger I cut, this new knife slice ran almost exactly along the old scar from that Scouting "ax accident." I think there might be an even deeper lesson here, but I will have to ponder it for awhile.

September 8, 2009

Good Students ASK Questions

There is a tendency among Asian students, Koreans in particular, to refrain from asking questions in class. It seems as though they have the opinion that to ask a question shows that you have not been listening carefully enough to the professor's lecture. So, since they do not want to appear disrespectful to their professors nor as unintelligent to their classmates, they simply do not ask questions in class. This is a problem for the teacher who sees education principally as the equipping of students with skills to ask hard questions about ideas, about others, and about themselves.

In the past, I have experienced this disinclination to questioning by some of the students within Fontbonne's International MBA program where I've taught for the past four summers. Since most of the international students at Fontbonne were Asian, I have not been surprised to find the same tendency among my students here at Handong. The challenge, as always for one who is called to teach, is to engage the thinking of my students. To call upon them and encourage them to ask questions. I knew it would be a difficult objective to attain. I realized that I would be lecturing to a classroom filled with respectful and attentive listeners. What I'm seeking, though, are actively engaged listeners who don't just drink in the lecture, but ones who ponder ideas and pose questions. So here at the beginning of my second week of teaching I still had only modest hopes of prompting maybe one or, at the most, two questions from each class. To my very pleased amazement, though, this morning's Survey of American Law lecture was interrupted by no less than 10 questions throughout the 75 minutes I spent with my 40 students. That's got to some sort of record! (Well, . . . maybe). It was great! One question from a student would prompt an explanation on my part, and then I would follow it up with a question of my own back to the student -- not to put them on the spot, but to encourage them to think about the question they had asked and then, to encourage them to ask the next question, to go deeper, to think things through.

Some students already have a basic grasp on some elemental concepts of law, so they asked questions about issues such as "double jeopardy" and "procedural bar." Others simply needed a better explanation of the definition of the technical legal terms that were being used -- such as "jurisdiction" What was amazing, though, was the fact that they were doing just what I have been inviting and encouraging them to do -- Asking Questions! Jesus did it when he was but a boy of twelve. Take a look at Luke 2:46-47. During his time of ministry, one of his principle means of instruction was asking questions. Probably the ancient teacher who is best known for instructing by means of posing questions is Socrates. In fact, the "Socratic Method" is still practiced by professors in most first year law school classes throughout the United States. Posing questions to students is one of the most effective ways to train them to think and to equip them to ask questions themselves. To pose and ponder the persistent questions of life -- I believe that's what the Apostle Paul was exhorting his readers to do when he wrote:

"Test [i.e. Examine or Question] everything; hold fast what is good"
(1 Thessalonians 5:21)

My students at Fontbonne and MBU heard that phrase as the last words from my mouth during every class lecture or discussion. Just like them, all of my new students at Handong will hear it as the concluding words of each class I teach.

September 10, 2009

Striving to Live a Balanced Life

One of my biggest weaknesses, according to my family and friends, is my tendency to say "Yes" when asked to take on a new task. Their counsel often comes in the words: "You need to say "No" more often!" I am now -- just a little shy of three weeks into my visiting professorship -- beginning to face making decisions in response to requests for my service.

It happened Tuesday evening this week. The UIL (U.S. & International Law) student organization held its first meeting of the semester. Prof. Kim presided over introductions of the faculty. Being the only American professor teaching in the UIL program I was asked to serve as an advisor to the students who are hoping to continue their legal studies in the States after graduating from HGU. Such a request, though, is not out the ordinary range of duties for a professor and I don't anticipate that it will require a great deal of my time outside of normal office hours. At this point, advising students is within the balance. The following day, however, I was invited to yet another meeting of the undergraduate law students. This one -- combing both UIL and Korean Law students -- is planned for Friday evening. Supper will be provided! Only one problem, though. I had already accepted an invitation to attend a gathering sponsored by HIC (Handong International Church) at Chilpo Beach this Friday evening. There's going to be a bonfire! I was even asked to help prepare and tend to the bonfire.

Those of you who know me well know how hard it is for me to resist a request to help build a fire. So, you know where I'll be this Friday. Even though Prof. Kim suggested to me at lunch today that it would be best if I could attend both events at least for a short time. Evidently the Korean faculty here has developed the ability to be in two places at the same time. I, on the other hand, have not. Looks like I am clearly in need of Ninja training. I'm pretty sure that this will lead to imbalance in my life, so at this point, I'm resisting. The requests this week, however, didn't end there. After Student Chapel Wednesday afternoon, the Church Administrator for HIC approached me and asked if I might consider becoming a Life Group leader. The leader's duties include hosting a small group Bible Study, prayer and worship time at least once every other week. They would leave it up to me to define the make-up of the group such as spoken language ability, age, gender, interests, major field of study, etc. I'm praying about this one. Its within the scope of my primary gift -- pastor-teacher.

Then comes the final request -- presented to me at today law school faculty lunch meeting. I was informed that the Korean faculty is in the process of writing a textbook covering an introduction to Korean Law. Here's where I come in -- they're intending to publish this book in English. None of the faculty, though, speaks English as a first language -- except . . . me. So I've been "asked" to serve as the general editor of the textbook project. This one is more difficult to decline. Its within the board scope of my employment contract, so it looks like I'll be doing some editing later this semester. I'm not certain when the project is scheduled for completion, but I got the distinct impression that they would like to have it done before the beginning of the new semester next year. The one redeeming aspect of this project is that I can only do the editing work on chapters that have first been submitted to me by my colleagues. I'll have to wait and see what I'll get. After all these requests for my service, I was quite pleased to accept Prof. Kuyper Lee's invitation to take a walk after lunch today along with Prof. Kim and Prof.

Chang. Prof. Lee has a habit of taking an afternoon walk following lunch. Unlike the American professors at Handong who I've been walking with in the evening, my Korean brothers don't walk the road around campus. Instead, they follow a path into the wooded hills that extend to the west of campus just beyond All Nations Hall, our new building. Once we were well upon the trail, I remembered that this was a pathway that I had hiked on a couple of occasions during my brief stay at Handong in the summer of '04. Prof. Lee, however, led us along the path to where it joined a "less traveled" road up a hill to an overlook. The sight was astounding with a wonderful view to the east. We could even see a portion of Pohang harbor! The site itself was a beautifully manicured hillside with a large mound of earth about 10 feet in diameter at its center. Prof. Lee explained to me that it was a family burial plot. It provided a wonderful place to rest and reflect -- upon life and death; work and rest; requests and responses -- to reflect upon how best to live a balanced life. I think I'll be returning to this sacred place many times. I believe my visits here will help to keep me in balance.

September 11, 2009

He Causes the Rain to Fall . . .

Friday afternoon I faced a dilemma. I had committed to help build a bonfire for the HIC outing to Chilpo Beach, but as I was finishing up some work in my office, Prof. Kim, my Department Chair, walked in and sat down. With a serious look on his face, he explained that the law student meeting planned for this evening was a very important meeting -- the first of the semester. He appealed to me requesting again that I come to this meeting, as he had done yesterday at our faculty luncheon. He very much wanted to introduce me to the Korean law students.

You see, the undergraduate School of Law is made up of both UIL majors (those studying U.S. and International Law) and Korean Law majors. The students studying Korean Law are planning to become lawyers in Korea or possibly Civil Servants with the government. According to Prof. Kim, the Korean law students have not associated very well with the UIL students in the past. He is hoping that my presence on the UIL faculty along with the addition of Prof. Chang (who, though he is a Korean national, earned two law degrees at Cornell Law School in New York) will help to bring the undergraduate law students together.

The pressure was on! I'm beginning to understand how Koreans try to persuade you to comply with their requests. What was I to do? I told Prof. Kim that I would go and speak with the young man from HIC (the international church on campus) to whom I had committed my help in building the bonfire. I said that I would explain my situation to him and see if I could still help prepare for the fire and come to the law student meeting a little later on. I was trying to figure out a way to be in two places at the same time. The Lord intervened, though. As I was helping Kris load firewood into the back of the church van, it began to rain. About half-way through the loading process, Kris got a call on his mobile. It was Pastor Dave informing him that the bonfire outing had been cancelled due to the rain. Kris and I had had a good time talking while working together. But now, I was at liberty to take the walk across campus to my hermitage, change my shirt and head back to Nehemiah Hall where the law student meeting was just beginning. When I arrived, I was heartily greeted by Prof. Kim, and my TA, Mr. Mok. I was pleasantly surprised to find that the students had even prepared a place at one of the tables for me with my name in Korean, no less!

I was tremendously encouraged by the Korean law students who sat with me at our table. Each one introduced himself and spoke of how they were seeking God's guidance for their futures. One young man who introduced himself by his English name "David J.

Sparrow" even quoted one of his favorite Bible verses: "The heart of man plans his way, but the Lord directs his steps." He said he was confident that God would direct him in through his education and into his career. All in all, the evening was a true blessing. I'm completely exhausted and needing to get my rest. But, it is wonderful to see how God does indeed direct our steps and enable us to live a balanced life as we yield to Him and seek to serve others. So, good night! May you rest well and rise tomorrow to learn more of His faithfulness that is new every morning!

September 14, 2009

The Day with Others - The Day Alone

Bonhoeffer writes in Life Together that living in community is a balance between the day with others and the day alone -- between communion and solitude. Beyond the challenges of responding to the demands upon my time, I'm finding that a deeper part of living a balanced life is understanding more of what Brother Bonhoeffer is teaching and then, putting it into better practice. There is a sense of community here at Handong that I don't believe I have ever experienced before. Possibly it is the fact that nearly all of my daily experiences transpire within close proximity of others on the campus -- or just maybe -- there is truly something about the spirit of the students and faculty here that forms community.

This was impressed upon me again this morning when one of the students I had met last Friday evening, David J. Sparrow, greeted me as I walked across campus. He was sipping a morning coffee on his way to a 10am lecture. I noticed that he looked a bit weary already at mid-morning on Monday. He explained that he had been up at 5 to gather with other students for prayer. That's the spirit of these students! Nearly every evening you can hear groups singing together -- sometimes their singing goes on late into the night. Sundays are especially full of opportunities to experience the day with others. Since I've been here, I have been invited each

Sunday to attend an international service with the Enlow family at one of the local churches in downtown Pohang.

While the entire congregation of Joyful Church is quite large, the gathering of internationals who meet in the afternoon numbers only about 50. They are a wonderful group of believers from many countries throughout the world. The hymns and songs are sung heartily. Our worship leader is from Liverpool, England (and everybody from Liverpool can sing!). Eric is primarily responsible for the preaching portion of the service. He's been going through an encouraging series on the Covenants. I've not only been attending the afternoon services with the Enlow's, though. There is a wonderful church gathering right here on campus each Sunday morning at 9.

The folks at Handong International Church are a wonderful worshipping community, too! Attending both the morning service on campus and then afternoon services in Pohang makes for a very full day with others. Since I don't have Sandy with me now, I'm inclined to spend as much time with other believers on Sunday's as I can. Sunday evenings then bring me time in the day alone. Yesterday, I spent the time writing my son Caleb and my daughter-in-law Micaela a hand-written letter which I posted via airmail this morning. I'm realizing afresh a lesson that Caleb has reminded me of several times in the past -- a hand-written letter can be an especially strong means of encouragement to others. Even the Apostle Paul emphasized this truth through his own letters to the Christians in the local churches he had helped to plant. (Galatians 6:11).

The day with others -- the day alone: a balance of community and solitude, conversation and prayer, service and rest, singing and silence. I'm hoping that I will be able to experience the fullness of this balance in life in greater ways during the coming months this fall.

September 15, 2009

A Hike into the Hills above Handong

Robert Frost famously wrote:

Two roads diverged in a yellow wood,
And sorry I could not travel both
And be one traveler, long I stood
And looked down one as far as I could
To where it bent in the undergrowth;

Then took the other, as just as fair,
And having perhaps the better claim,
Because it was grassy and wanted wear;
Though as for that the passing there
Had worn them really about the same,

And both that morning equally lay
In leaves no step had trodden black.
Oh, I kept the first for another day!
Yet knowing how way leads on to way,
I doubted if I should ever come back.

I shall be telling this with a sigh
Somewhere ages and ages hence:
Two roads diverged in a wood, and I—
I took the one less traveled by,
And that has made all the difference.

The words of Frost have taken on new meaning for me over the past few months. Choosing to accept the call to teach here at Handong was definitely a new stage in my journey along the road less traveled by, though some may say, I've been on that road for more than a few months or even years. I'll let others judge that as they observe and evaluate the path I've taken. This morning Frost's words came to mind in a fresh way as I took a hike up along the paths shown to me last week by Professor Kuyper Lee. I was trying to find my way back to that beautiful overlook, and as I walked I encountered several diverging roads -- some well trodden and others less traveled. It was a bit of a challenge since I was walking the trail not from where we had started the first time, but from where we ended-up.

I can hear a few of you saying, "There he goes again, walking the opposite direction -- against the flow." I guess it would have been a whole lot easier to have gone back the same way I had been led before, but something prompted me to take the road we had returned upon. As I did, though, I started to notice some "signs" along the way -- not actual road signs, but a pile of old bamboo beside the path at one point, and then a cultivated field a bit farther up the hill, and even another grave site just before I reached the top of the hill and the clearing where the burial mound was situated. The view to the east was a bit hazy, but still beautiful. I followed Socrates' example and took time to pause and think. It is a special place quite conducive to thinking -- to pondering -- to reflecting. I think it has now become to me my first sacred place here in Korea.

On the hike back down toward campus, I took the path back along the way upon which I had first been led to this place. It was also a path "whose leaves have not been trodden black." I'm thinking I should get up even earlier next time -- before the dawn -- and return to the overlook to watch the sunrise. Maybe in a few days, though, as it is getting cooler each night now, and the mornings are brisk. Some of the trees are even beginning to turn their fall colors. Each day my surroundings are becoming more of a yellow wood, and it reminds me to continue the journey along the road less traveled by.

September 16, 2009

Uni[ty-in-Di]versity

One of the most striking differences between my experiences in the past on American university campuses and those here at Handong is the multitude of languages I hear spoken on any given day. When just taking a walk from my apartment to All Nations Hall, it is not usual for me to hear no less than four or five different languages being spoken by students and faculty, alike. While Korean is by far the most common language here, I also hear Swahili spoken by students from Congo, Khmer by students from Cambodia, Dari (a dialect of Persian) and Pashto by students from Afghanistan, as well as Russian and Mongolian by students and German by a couple of faculty members, just to name a few. Yesterday afternoon Handong's multitude of languages was impressed upon me in a new way. Each Wednesday at 3:15pm, students gather for an English chapel service. Though English is the unifying language of this gathering, there comes a time in the service when the worship leader asks the congregation to sing, or sometimes to pray, in the languages of each one's homeland. To some observers this might have sounded like a cacophony. As I sat and listened, though, I began to discern the various individual languages, and while I did not understand the particular meaning of each, I realized that those who spoke were joining together with all present in words of praise and thanksgiving to God. While there was a diversity of expression, there was unity of purpose. Then a passage from Revelation came to mind: *"After this I looked, and behold, a great multitude that no one could number, from every nation, from all tribes and peoples and languages, standing before the throne and before the Lamb, clothed in white robes, with palm branches in their hands."* (Revelation 7:9)

September 19, 2009

Fun & Games

Many of you may have the impression from my earlier posts that the students here at Handong are all quite serious and diligent and spend their days studying and going to class, and if they're not in class or in the library, then you might well think that they are either in small group Bible study, singing in a choir or quietly doing their personal devotions. Well, they are committed students, no doubt -- But, they also know how to enjoy a little fun and a few games. Today was a great example -- the annual "HILS Cup Challenge" for the international law school students was being waged. Throughout the entire morning the students composing four teams engaged in a variety of conventional and unconventional games as they competed for the prized "HILS Cup." They played basketball and ran funny relays, pouring water into bottles atop the heads of their teammates, and then finished the day with a major tug-of-war. While the international law students were competing for "HILS Cup" on the courts, some other Handong students were engaged in a full-scale soccer match on the pitch in front of the Student Union. I paused to watch their game for a while and came away convinced that some of the players' skills might well qualify them for FIFA! So, I trust I have now corrected the record and cleared-up any inaccurate impressions I may have given in the past posts. Handong students work, worship, rest and play -- They're living well-balanced lives.

September 23, 2009

Keep Your Head Warm and Your Feet Dry

Autumn has arrived, and with it, a light, gentle, steady rain this morning. Cooler temperatures and damper days are upon us. I've started wearing my jacket, and I'm reminded of some very basic instructions given me by my mother: "Always keep your head warm and your feet dry." Without a doubt, taking heed to those words is one of the surest ways to ward off the coughs and colds that all too frequently tend to plague fall days and nights. I, however, was doing neither earlier today. There I was walking across campus in the rain without an umbrella -- my hair collecting the raindrops and my shoes beginning to soak in the moisture. When I made it to my office, Mr. Mok (who usually arrives quite early) recognized my dilemma and readily offered me the use of his umbrella for the day. I assured him that I would head directly for the campus store on my way to lunch and purchased one of my own. And, I did. I purchased the largest and strongest umbrella that was available. Mr. Mok recommended one like his that holds-up well in high winds, which he advises me are quite common here in the foothills above the seashore. So, I'm now equipped to do a somewhat better job at keeping my head warm and my feet dry. Its afternoon and the rain has passed, though the skies are still overcast -- a bit of a gloomy day. Looks like I'll need to keep that jacket and umbrella handy, and in fact, with the increased likelihood of rain that appears to have now set in for these fall days, I guess I'll even pull out my old wool cap from Dublin. You might not naturally think it, but Ireland and Korea do share a few things in common.

September 24, 2009

My First Taste of Kimchi

Put a star on the calendar. I did it! In spite of deep personal reservations over trying any sort of new or different food (especially one that does not have the most pleasant of aromas -- I know, you thought I was the adventurous type; well, I am when it comes to new places, but I'm not when it comes to new tastes), in spite of all that, I did it. I finally took my first bite of kimchi at lunch today with my Korean colleagues. The undergraduate law faculty (among whom I am the only American) had been kind enough to select a restaurant for our weekly lunch meeting that specialized in a beef broth soup -- They didn't tell me, though, that the "beef" parts were, for the most part, unidentifiable cuts of some internal organs (I think -- I hope). The darker pieces of beef actually tasted a bit like small cuts of roast, but the lighter chunks were slices of stomach, I'm told. I didn't eat them. The soup broth was quite tasty, though, and with a spoonful of rice, the combination was actually hearty.

So after a few healthy helpings of the beef soup, I picked up my chopsticks (yes, I'm actually getting the hang of them) and reached over the table and nabbed my first portion of kimchi. It was made from several varieties of lettuce and cabbage mixed together. It looked a lot like a tossed salad with a bunch of red dressing and flakes of red pepper. Maybe it was my seasonal congestion, but for whatever reason, I could not sense the distinctive aroma as potently as I had on prior occasions. Maybe this was a "mild" kimchi. In any case, I dropped the collection in my little white dish (sort of your own serving plate) and then selected a smaller portion and quickly popped it in my mouth. No, I didn't hold my nose! I was told by some other American that holding one's nose on your first experience with kimchi didn't really "count"! Anyhow, I had enough nasal congestion today to serve as a shield, but once I had the kimchi in my mouth, I began to sense its aromatic effects. Within moments my sinuses were opening and the flavors proceeded to play upon my palate. Wait a minute -- this isn't all that bad! In fact, its pretty good. Good enough for several more bites.

Although I still feel very much like a stranger here, I think I may have taken a significant step in my journey to learn more of what it means to live in community with my Korean brothers and sisters. Food, in certain ways, does indeed form community. And a willingness to eat the food that characterizes a culture brings one into a deeper realization and practice of community.

September 26, 2009

Befuddled by Bowing

I've found that some of my expectations in coming to Handong, those that I had formed mainly from recollections of my experiences here in the summer of 2004, were mistaken or, at best, confused. One of those expectations was that the students and the faculty at Handong possessed a greater sense of genuine commitment to the things that matter in life -- God, others, justice, mercy and peace. There's no doubt that I have found an enthusiasm among the students and most faculty, but what I'm beginning to think is that the zeal I'm seeing and hearing in many (though, I'm sure not all) is more "worked-up" than "grown-up" -- more like an "event enthusiasm" than a genuine way of looking at life born from experiences that challenge our faith and cultivate hope in God rather than in ourselves. One of the most telling signs of this enthusiasm is the outward respect shown by the students to their teachers. I recall once when I was walking across campus on my first visit here five years ago that I was completely caught off guard when two students who were approaching me on the sidewalk literally stopped and simultaneously bowed to me. I wasn't even wearing a coat and tie! I was in shorts and a t-shirt, yet they still saw me as an American professor and so reacted with an outward show of respect that this culture cultivates.

Now that I've returned and have been here for five weeks, I still see students bowing to their professors. It puzzled me at first. How was I to respond? Do you just smile and accept the cultural "homage" or is it appropriate for me to bow in return? I felt uneasy just standing there or walking on without acknowledging the student who had bowed. So, I've been bowing back -- trying to express my respect for them. What I've noticed, though, is that the bow is not so much an expression of respect or recognition as it was the Korean version of our polite greeting: "How are you?"

Most who offer that greeting to others are not really listening for a response as they are expecting merely to hear the routine "Fine, and you?" We pass each other with these greetings, but rarely do we listen for words that reveal. We're too focused on pursuing our own path to be interrupted by others.

You would think, though, that a bow would prompt you to pause -- to reflect -- to actually see the other person. Yet, while there is an "enthusiasm" about showing outward respect to others and even to God through the many worship services and the informal gatherings for praise, worship and prayer -- the bowing that is going on seems to be more a show for others to see that I'm doing what is expected of me than a genuine expression of heart and mind. Maybe after five weeks I'm just beginning to wake up from the illusions that I've had about life here. Maybe what I'm actually realizing is that people here are the same as people everywhere. We all struggle with wearing masks so that others only see what we want them to see -- what we think they expect to see from us. We all need to admit that we're just putting on the mask for the day -- we all need (as Michael Card sings) to pray for the grace to tear off the mask and see the art of our face.

Bowing is a good thing whether the one bowing is just bowing on the outside and not on the inside or whether the bow is indeed sincere. I think it is, at a minimum, a step in the right direction. I'm hoping that I will become more deliberate about my bowing -- truly seeing the other person and becoming, I hope, more concerned about the things that really matter in life. May God continue, in each day, to write the poem of our lives even through disappointments and mistaken expectations.

September 28, 2009

Do Looks or Books Make the Man???

C.S. Lewis wrote in his essay "On the Reading of Old Books" that for every new book one reads, one should read an old book, or if that is too difficult, at least one old book for every three new. From Lewis' perspective the old books help us to see what our contemporary eyes are blinded to. We need the insights of the earlier days, or what others have called "the wisdom of the ages," to give us broader views and deeper understandings of the challenges of life and what it means to be truly human. Lewis, I believe we may say, would strongly argue for the proposition that books make the man. There is within Korean culture, however, a strong predilection (I'm beginning to find) that looks are what make the man. The Korean man views himself as "the Italian of East Asia" - suave, debonair, passionate. (No kidding! That is actually a quote I've heard from more than one Korean man who has tried to explain to me just how Koreans are distinct from other East Asians). As you might imagine, such a view has more than a little tendency to clash with Lewis' notion of the making of a man. While Christians in Korea attempt to balance the two views by stressing the importance of learning, there is yet a strong inclination towards what Billy Crystal's character "Fernando Marvelous" embodied in his memorable turn of phrase: "It is better to look good than to feel good." Really, could there be two more polar opposites that C.S. Lewis and Fernando?

So what does this have to do with an American trying to teach in Korea? Well, when students and some fellow faculty, for that matter, are as much or more concerned about "looking good" as they are about "learning good" you come face-to-face with a definite challenge. I don't know that I can say that this challenge to one's personal formation is peculiar to Asian culture -- there are, I would venture to say, plenty of Americans consumed with "looking good" as the highest good -- but emphasis upon the external appears to have an Asian twist that I feel I have not even yet begun to understand. I'm hoping, though, that tomorrow will bring more opportunities to seek first to understand those into whose culture I've come before I start evaluating them from my perspective. Tomorrow, I expecting, will bring more occasions to read some old books when my cargo of 9 boxes are finally delivered. I've been anxiously awaiting their arrival for several weeks. I had received a call from the custom agent's office in Seoul about 10 days ago and requested a copy of my passport. I assumed that they wanted to verify that I had been issued an E-1 visa (granted only to professors).

Upon receipt of my fax, they assured me that the shipment was due in port on 27 Sep and that they expected it to clear customs easily since the cargo was not for commercial (books that would be sold) but was intended for educational purposes. I even got the impression that the lady at the custom agent's office knew about Handong and was trying to help me get my books as soon as possible. Then came the second call. They now needed a letter from me explaining that the books would not be sold, but would be used in my teaching at Handong. Thankfully, my teaching assistant, Mr. Mok, was able to draft up a quick letter in Korean that set forth the requisite affirmations of use. I had no idea what I was signing since the letter was written in Korean, but I have come to trust Mr. Mok implicitly for all my needs. I knew he understood how much I have been looking forward to getting my books, and more than that, I think he, though being very much a young Korean man, is persuaded that books rather than looks truly make the man.

And with those 500 pounds of books I trusting will come the means that I need to sharpen my sensitivity, to hone my hearing, to refine my reflections on life and on learning in this new land. At this stage of life, I don't have much hope in "looks" but I do have a great expectation in "books" and in particular "the Book" making the man. So we do not lose heart. Though our outer self is wasting away, our inner self is being renewed day by day. For this light momentary affliction is preparing for us an eternal weight of glory beyond all comparison, as we look not to the things that are seen but to the things that are unseen. For the things that are seen are transient, but the things that are unseen are eternal. (2 Corinthians 4:16-18)

6

October 1, 2009

Six Degrees of Separation or is it Just Two?

Some years back an idea was popularized by a party game called something like "Six Degrees of Separation from Kevin Bacon." The idea is that all of us are connected to everyone else in the world by no more than six paths of life experiences with other people. In short, this theory holds that any two people in the world may be connected to each other by learning that the first person (A) knows someone (1) who knows someone(2) who knows someone (3) who knows someone (4) who knows someone (5) who, in turn, knows the second person (6).

In sociological terms, the idea is called "the small world phenomenon." The notion was explored through several experiments conducted by Stanley Milgram examining the average path length for social networks of people in the United States. The research was groundbreaking in that it suggested that human society is a small world type network characterized by short path lengths. While these experiments are often associated with the phrase "six degrees of separation", Milgram did not use that term himself. (Read more) The notion that we live in a small world is illustrated in this diagram that demonstrates the lines of connections. I've actually thought that the better focal point for the small world phenomenon would in fact be my good friend, Rich Cartier, not Kevin Bacon. In my experience, at least, nearly every time I've been with Cartier, and he has met some stranger, Cartier quickly discovered that he knew someone who the stranger also knew. Not six degrees, but only two! Well now, even in Korea I am discovering that it is indeed a small world even if you don't know Cartier!

Here's how this truth has been coming home to me at Handong. A few days ago, I started a small study group that meets in my office on Monday evenings each week. As I was speaking with one of the students named Esther, I learned that although she was Korean, she had grown up in the Philippines where her parents serve as missionaries. I thought that was interesting and mentioned to Esther that I knew some people who taught at a school in the Philippines called "Faith Academy." A smile came over Esther's face. She said she had graduated from Faith in Manila. I asked her if she knew Steve and Dottie St. Clair, and while she did not know the St. Clair's personally, she was aware of Faith Academy's Davao campus where Steve teaches.

I had come to know the St. Clair's through a local church (Grace Bible Chapel) in St. Louis where my family and I were in fellowship for a number of years. Steve and Dottie visited the church when they were in the States and during those visits I learned of their work at Faith. So, I think that qualifies as two degrees of separation or maybe, if we must be technical, three. I am getting closer though, Cartier!

Then the next day, I noticed a Westerner (that's usually how I initially describe non-Asians until I get to know them better) walking around campus who I had not yet met. When I crossed paths with her a second time in the same day, I introduced myself and asked Jean where she was from. She replied, "You mean originally?" I said, "How ever you would like to answer the question." She told me that she had been born and grew up in Northern Ireland, but spent 18 years living in a number of countries in Africa where she served with Wycliffe Bible Translators.

She was here at Handong teaching a linguistics class for three weeks. She now lived in the Philippines. The Philippines, you say -- I bet you think I then asked her if she knew the St. Clairs. I wish I had, but Jean's mention of Wycliffe brought to mind another couple that my family and I had also met during our years at Grace. So instead, I asked her if she knew Reg and Barb Naylor who serve with Wycliffe in Kathmandu, Nepal.

Once again, that familiar smile came over her face. It was a smile quite similar to the smile on Esther's face when I mentioned that I knew of her high school, Faith Academy. Jean knew of the Naylor's work in Nepal and it was evident that she considered them as outstanding fellow-workers in the mission to translate the Bible into the languages of the many still unreached people groups throughout the world. That's a definite demonstration of "two degrees"! So, I'm becoming more and more convinced that it truly is a small world; especially as we meet people with whom we are connected, first and foremost, through Christ our Savior and then with others through our service in and for the one, holy catholic (with a lower case "c") church and the world, both of which are growing smaller through diminishing degrees of separation.

October 6, 2009

Life is Short

One of my grandmother's most poignant sayings, according to my mother, was: "Old people have to die, but young people can die." I have endeavored to keep this timeless truth in mind even in my teaching. I follow Prof. Richard Hughes' example and seek, as one of my principle objectives in each class I teach, to convince my students that they are going to die.

I do this not to be morbid, but instead to urge my students always to remember that we are limited beings; to remind them that each of us is here upon this earth for only a brief time. In the words of wise Solomon, our lives are but a breath, a mist that rises in the morning and soon disappears. The ancient Roman teacher Seneca spoke similarly to his students:

> "You are living as if destined to live for ever; your own frailty never occurs to you; you don't notice how much time has already passed, but squander it as though you had a full and overflowing supply -- though all the while that very day which you are devoting to somebody or something may be your last. You act like mortals in all that you fear, and like immortals in all that you desire."

I had only last week reminded my students of the brevity of life and the certainty of death, but when I spoke those few words I had no idea that their concreteness would be brought home to the Handong community so soon. It was just this past Saturday when nearly all of the students and faculty were away from campus with their families celebrating the Korean Thanksgiving -- the fall festival called Chuseok -- that a few students remained around campus. Saturday afternoon the weather was balmy. Three Korean students, all upperclassmen looking forward to graduation in the coming months, decided to take a walk along Chilpo Beach after lunch.

As they walked along the sandy shore a large wave suddenly rushed in upon them and pulled them out toward the sea. Two were able to hold on to one another and make their way back to the shore. The third, though, could not overcome the undertow and was pulled into the deeper waters where tragically he drown. I learned of the student's death from my teaching assistant, Mr. Mok. Younghoon was a close friend of the young man. They both started their studies here at Handong together in the same small group and had become good friends over the years. Younghoon told me that he had received a call from his friend just two hours before he took his walk with his two companions along the beach.

I cannot begin to describe the somberness that has settled upon this campus. Students and faculty alike are pondering the brevity of life. In my classes this week, I've urged my students thoughtfully to reflect upon Moses' words in Psalm 90. "So teach us to number our days that we may get a heart of wisdom."

October 8, 2009

Zeal Without Knowledge

It is not good to have zeal without knowledge, nor to be hasty and miss the way. (Proverbs 19:2)

Most university students are interested in acquiring knowledge, but they often don't have much zeal for the effort it takes to gain it. Similarly, most professors are concerned about imparting knowledge, but some often lack a certain enthusiasm in fulfilling this calling. My experience here at Handong over the past seven weeks, however, has confronted me with somewhat the opposite dilemma. Not a lack of enthusiasm on the part of students or professors, but what I can only describe at this point as an over abundance of zeal. There is an intensity about experiential events -- prayer meetings, praise and worship times and chapel services. Emotions run high nearly all the time. There are expressions of great joy and then, on other occasions, deep sorrow.

The zeal demonstrated by so many here is both heart-warming and challenging. There is obviously a great desire to live life to the fullest in every respect. My concern, though, is that the zeal I see in students, and even in some faculty, is a zeal that lacks a balancing pursuit for and value of knowledge. It is a zeal that is all-consuming yet, it appears, in my limited capacity to perceive, to be not well-founded in truth. Not that I have any better handle on the truth than any other humble seeker who is, like all humans, both finite and fallen. Yet, there is a warning in Solomon's words. It is not good to have zeal without knowledge, nor to be hasty and miss the way.

Just this morning I ran across a note I had made some years ago when reading Thomas Merton's autobiography. I think Merton aptly expresses the way our desires, our zeal can impinge upon our pursuit of knowledge and understanding:

> I think that if there is one truth that people need to learn, in the world, especially today, it is this: The intellect is only theoretically independent of desire and appetite in ordinary, actual practice. It is constantly being blinded and perverted by the ends and aims of passion, and the evidence it presents to us with such a show of impartiality and objectivity is fraught with interest and propaganda. We have become marvelous at self-delusion; all the more so, because we have gone to such trouble to convince ourselves of our own absolute infallibility.
>
> The desires of the flesh -- and by that I mean not only sinful desires, but even the ordinary, normal appetites for comfort and ease and human respect, are fruitful sources of every kind of error and misjudgment, and because we have these yearnings in us, our intellects (which, if they operated all alone in a vacuum, would indeed, register with pure impartially what they saw) present to us everything distorted and accommodated to the norms of our desire. (Seven Story Mountain, p. 225)

I'm beginning to sense that an important part of my task here is to learn how I might better balance my natural inclination to pursue knowledge with an authentic zeal that is born out of desire cultivated by hope in the promise of the educational endeavor. That promise is that education can and does occur, even though we who seek to teach others are so fraught with failures and misunderstandings. Education is not the mere acquisition of knowledge and skills to better one's earning power. It is not "learning to earn" a better living. Rather, it is learning to live a better life. Education is the formation of a whole, complete person challenged by a sense of calling, equipped with skills for engaging ideas and focused on serving others – a person whose zeal is tempered by knowledge, but whose knowledge is put to use through love in the service of others.

"Knowledge [alone] puffs up, but love builds up." (1 Corinthians 8:1)

October 13, 2009

The Beat of Drums and Clash of Cymbals

I have been told that it often takes some time to grow accustomed to a new culture, a new country, a new community. Often usual customs of the local people present challenges to one unaccustomed to their practices. One such custom here in Korea is the playing of traditional drums and cymbals. In a few weeks, the students of Handong will celebrate a festival. One of the highlights of the festival is traditional drumming, cymbals and the accompanying dance.

In order to prepare for this festival, a group of about 20 students have begun practicing the drumming and cymbal crashing outside the back of the Student Center under the large canopy. The structure of the Student Center forms sort of an amphitheater that resonates any sounds that are produced within it. This effect becomes particularly reverberating when the drum and cymbal corp commence there rehearsal. It started last evening about 8pm. It continued -- constantly -- with the same recurring rhythm and clashing -- loud pounding -- and pronounced clashing -- until after 11pm. My apartment in the Mission House is within 100 yards of the area of the Student Center where the "rehearsal" was taking place. Needless to say, I was not able to even think about sleep until after the numbing drumming and clashing cymbals ceased.

While I sat and listened to the recurring rhythms, I was reminded of a story that my son Caleb told me from his experiences living among the Yanomami Indians in the south of Venezuela. The young men of the community began preparing one night for a hunt. The preparation ritual involved their gathering around a large fire with drums and dancing. The partying continued to three days and nights before the young men (with Caleb tagging along) departed for the hunt.

As Caleb first reported this account in his email to us, he reminded us that teenagers are the same all over the world. They all enjoy the strong rhythms of the drum, dancing and a never-ending party. Well, Caleb's assessment of the young Yanomami seems to hold true for the youth of Korea also -- at least here on the campus of Handong. So evidently, I will need to adjust my sleeping schedule or pull out my trusty ear plugs (an item every world traveler needs to have readily at hand -- another lesson I've learned from my son Caleb). In any case, I am beginning, with a large measure of grace, to grow accustomed to their sound. I take some solace in knowing that even the Lord enjoins his congregation to:

Praise him with tambourine and dance;
Praise him with strings and pipe!
Praise him with sounding cymbals;
Praise him with loud clashing cymbals!
(Psalm 150:4-5)

October 16, 2009

Is There a Universal Language?

Is there a medium of communication understood by all humans? How about all living beings? Is there a way of conveying meaning to others that can be apprehended by others no matter where you are or with whom you are? For a stranger, a foreigner, an alien in a strange, foreign and alien land this is a persistent question -- a question that keeps coming back and confronting you in the face of your on-going life experiences. When your TA ("Teaching Assistant" which also means for me, "Translation Assistant") is not at your side, you quickly reach the point where you are desperately searching for a medium of common communication -- a universal means of conveying meaning. My nine weeks here in Korea have convinced me that the answer to this perplexing question is not found in any naturally spoken human language -- that's right, not even Esperanto!

What I'm finding, though, is that there is a universal language, and it is the universe itself. Those things in the universe around us -- both near by in nature and far out in space -- we see, we hear, we apprehend (and by we I mean all humans no matter your country of citizen or ethnicity) what all of us need to see, to hear, to apprehend. And, by looking and listening to what surrounds us all and what we all share, we can experience a common means of communication. One of the best examples of this universal reality is music -- and yes, some of you, my regular readers, may be asking right now, has the drum and cymbal corps begun another evening rehearsal? They have. -- But, it is not particular styles of music that I'm talking about, it is the human activity of making (or attempting to make)music that expresses this universality of meaning that is found in the universe itself.

Music is apart of the universe that is. Some have suggested that music is the artistic expression of the science of mathematics displaying the purpose, order and design that characterizes the universe that is. So, music may be one of the media for convey meaning and delight to ourselves and to others. True enough, you may respond that music as an expression may display dissonance and irresolution.

There is, though, music that will attract and delight humans no matter what their culture may be. It is music that displays the wonder of the universe in the same way that a glorious sunset delights all who witness it. It is music that expresses the wonder of life even as a blooming flower or the autumn blaze of colors across a hardwood valley. I hear this music in the songs that resonate through Handong's halls and hills.

> *The heavens declare the glory of God, and the sky above proclaims his handiwork.*
> *Day to day pours out speech and night to night reveals knowledge.*
> *There is no speech, nor are there words, whose voice is not heard.*
> *Their voice goes out through all the earth and their words to the end of the world.* (Psalm 19:1-4)

October 18, 2009

Consider the Birds of the Air . . . and also the Bugs Beneath

If we are instructed to consider the birds of the air and by so considering them, learn some of the most basic and important lessons of life, it would seem to be appropriate to re-direct this process of observation and learning from the skies overhead to the dirt beneath our feet. And, as birds inhabit the air above us, so too do insects thrive upon the grass and ground below.

Which insect would you think I see most often as I walk across campus and hike up into the hills surrounding Handong? Let's make this a multiple-choice question (that's what most of my students here are most happy to find on their examination papers). Would you say it is a(n):

A) Ant
B) Beetle
C) Butterfly
D) Dragonfly
E) Praying Mantis
F) Some other insect

Okay ... I threw that last choice in for fun just to start you thinking about how many other kinds of insects you could name. So now that I've narrowed the choices to five, which one do you think is most common in these parts of Korea at this time of the year? As I recall my experiences in high school biology, I remember how I searched fields and hills alike for large variety of insects during September and October in Missouri so that I might fill a large display box. The most prominent insect in my Missouri collection of autumn insects was the butterfly -- probably about six or seven different species, as well as a few moths for good measure. I always loved the butterflies, not only for their diverse designs of beauty, but also because of their formation through metamorphosis. They are a constant reminder that beauty arises out of the most unexpected of conditions and the most unlikely of characteristics.

So, with this past experience to guide me, wouldn't it seem most likely that the most common insects that I might find here would also be butterflies? You would think so; I thought so, but my experiences have proven different. I have seen a few butterflies and even more beetles, but the most common sights of all, nearly every day as I walk about, are the abundance of dragonflies! There are literally everywhere.

It may very well be that the autumn is one of the seasons when dragonflies mate. I don't know; I have some research to do on that. But, the question that presents itself to me is: what life lesson do the dragonflies teach? I'm pondering that one. Initially, I've observed that I rarely see just one dragonfly. I nearly always see two, three or more dragonflies in close proximity to one another. That would seem to remind us of the importance of community -- of life together with others. And, by the way, which of the five do you think is the insect I've observed most often after the dragonflies?

October 20, 2009

An Evening in Daegu

I don't "get out" much these days since I am, in many ways, nearly cloistered off in a hermitage when not teaching in the classroom or preparing to teach while in my study (a much better term than "office" to describe the space in which I do my work here). But there are a few occasions for some broader cultural enrichment. One of those opportunities came this past weekend when I accompanied Abraham Lee, Director of the University's Office of International Affairs (that's Abraham on the far left in our little group photo), his staff and three international students to a musical performance at a newly constructed opera house on the campus of one of Handong's sister universities located in the city of Daegu -- about a one hour drive from Pohang.

It proved to be a delightful evening at the theater. The performance was Jekyll and Hyde, the musical. The acting troop was from the States so everything -- dialogue and songs -- was in English! Though I was familiar with the plot line from Robert Louis Stevenson's novel, I was quite pleasantly surprised by the quality of the musical's script, set design and overall production.

On the whole, the performance was a powerful statement about the inadequacy of science to resolve the deepest problems facing humanity. Dr. Jekyll's scientific experiments could not overcome the struggles between good and evil within him. Indeed, apart from his pleas to God, Jekyll could not find an antidote against the human harm and deadly actions perpetrated by the evil Mr. Hyde. If the musical comes to the Fox in St. Louis, I would strongly recommend your attending and enjoying the performance as I did during a delightful evening in Daegu.

October 22, 2009

Halfway through and still Learning

Tuesday of this week marked the midway point in my first semester of teaching here at Handong. Time, indeed, does keep marching on. All the more need to take heed to Mr. Keating's maxim in Dead Poet's Society (one of my favorite films) -- Carpe Diem! If there is one continuing life lesson that is regularly impressed upon my thinking here, it is the importance of making the most of each opportunity that you are granted -- that's it: "To Seize the Day!"

And by that I mean not just in the sense of seizing the "big opportunity" to spend a year teaching abroad at a global university -- but even more so, to make the most of those "small opportunities" that come our way each day -- to answer a student's questions about seeking admission at a law school in the States; to write a letter in support of another student's application for a scholarship to a special international summer program in Norway; or, just to listen and give a few words of counsel and encouragement when my teaching assistant is expressing his concerns over the way he has been unfairly treated by another international faculty member.

I must confess. I still feel largely isolated here. No matter how much I have tried to assimilate into the international faculty and into the community of the university as a whole, it appears that I still end up spending large blocks of my time alone. This week, I even went over to Handong International Law School's (HILS) Wednesday chapel, but found that many of the students and most of the faculty do not attend this service since it is not required of them. The low attendance at this HILS midweek gathering reminded me somewhat of my own missed opportunities to attend daily worship in morning chapel services when I was studying at Concordia Seminary these past few years. Once I started going, I realized just how much I had indeed been missing of the formative experiences that shape us as a person both individually and in community.

One of the HILS faculty members who saw me walking up the hall commented, "Well, we just don't see you very much around here." (That's right, I'm on the undergraduate law faculty and my office is in another building and my classes are conducted on different floors from the elevated spaces of HILS). Then, I responded, "That's why I determined to be intentionally present at your chapel service today." He cringed and admitted that he would not be attending due to his heavy workload. (I thought that was the purpose of having a time of community worship in the middle of the work day -- to let your work be and acknowledge the One without whom nothing can be done! John 15:5 -- sorry, I've gone to preaching).

There are a few exceptions. Wednesday evening I was invited by my dear colleague Gayle to enjoy a grilled chicken salad with her. She's 73 and taught at University of California - Berkley for eight years as well as at a number of other lesser known institutions of higher learning throughout her long career. And now, although she is near the end of that long road, she decided to come to Korea and teach English at Handong this year. She really is an amazing woman! She is sort of the alter ego of Prof. S.K. Lee. Earlier in that day, I had asked Gayle if she might help me with my German studies and translation efforts. She was thrilled since her first degree is in German linguistics and she taught German for those eight years at Berkley. (I need to ask her when she was there; it might have been around the same time that Dr. Leary -- Timothy, that is -- was there, too). So now we have a regular meeting scheduled each Wednesday afternoon at 5. I'll need to have my lesson prepared and my translation in order. (Did I say what we would be translating from the German? -- Well, Bonhoeffer, of course! Letters and Papers from Prison).

So the semester is half-passed, and I'm still trying to find my way in this new world. Rather than having any big expectations of others, I simply need to trust each step to His continued guidance and, by His grace, make the most of each opportunity that I encounter along the way.

"My one command . . . is this: Listen to my voice, then I will be your God and you will be my people. In everything, follow the way that I mark out for you, and you shall have success." (Jeremiah 7:23)

October 25, 2009

Near Disaster . . . Averted

I've recently found that for me there are two things that definitely do not mix -- a microwave with its control panel labeled in Korean and watching a classic comedy film on your laptop across the room. Here's the scene, I had placed a packet of Orville Redenbacher's Gourmet Popping Corn (that I'd picked up last weekend in Daegu at the only Costco in this part of the country) in the microwave, punched a few buttons that I believed would provide sufficient time for the packet to pop, and then walked over to my laptop and searched out "Monty Python and the Holy Grail" on YouTube. It's quite amazing how engrossed a person can get into British humor! The film clip ran only 10 minutes, but that was more than enough time for my LG microwave to consume and nearly catch on fire that bag of Orville Redenbacher's! I had thought all would be well since the buttons I pushed had set the timer for only 6 minutes, 30 seconds. In my past experiences trying to pop corn in this particular microwave, I had pushed some buttons and it had taken a total of more than 6 1/2 minutes just to partially pop the packet.

What I did not realize, however, (it's a terrible thing when you can't speak or understand the language of those around you; it is even worse, though, when you cannot read that language) was that the buttons I had pushed before set the microwave to half power. What I had just pushed set the same amount of time but activated the maximum power that little LG can muster! While the bag was being micro waved, my attention was drawn deeper and deeper into Python-esque witty banter, and my hoots and howls of laughter were evidently drowning out any beeps or bells that the microwave was emitting.

It was not until I smelled the smoke and sensed that the room was filling with a denseness that I finally ran over to fling the microwave's door open, snatch the smoking bag just before it burst into flames and throw it into the sink where I doused it with water for a good three minutes. Once I was sure the bag was thoroughly extinguished, I opened windows in both back and front of the apartment (in spite of the cool fall temp's) and placed an oscillating fan on high in the middle of the room in a futile effort to exhaust the smoke that, by this time, had saturated the apartment and was beginning to infiltrate my neighbors' units.

Thankfully, no one else was around on Saturday night except the lone hermit who inhabits my room. Everyone else had much more interesting things to do than watch Monty Python on YouTube. Needless to say, I did not eat any popcorn while watching the remainder of the film. Instead, I was thankful that I was not cleaning up a much better mess, and even more grateful that my near disaster had been graciously averted.

October 27, 2009

Be Ready to be Interrupted

I've been slowly re-reading Bonhoeffer's *Life Together* over the past few weeks, and just encountered this admonition:

> We must be ready to allow ourselves to be interrupted by God. God will be constantly crossing our paths and canceling our plans by sending us people with claims and petitions. We may pass them by, preoccupied with our more important tasks, as the priest passed by the man who had fallen among thieves, perhaps -- reading the Bible. When we do that we pass by the visible sign of the Cross raised athwart our path to show us that, not our way, but God's way must be done.

I've only been here a little more than two months, but I've already developed plans and even, in many cases, such a tight schedule that when something interrupts, I'm quickly put-off. I wish I could say that I've acquired a deeper mindfulness of others while among my brothers and sister here in the East, but sadly my German-rooted-ness (not rudeness, but rooted-ness) still seems to be quite dominant in my fixing objectives for each day that too often leave little room for anything or anyone who is not "on the schedule."

Life is not smoother when you allow for interruptions -- you may find yourself walking across campus (as I did yesterday) only to hear your name being called by a student running up to you from behind. He then follows on closely the entire way to your office all the while throughout the course of your journey peppering you with questions about his future interests in international human rights advocacy.

Then, continuing his inquiries, he remains engaged in conversation with you for nearly as long as you had thought it would take to complete the composition of the exam you are scheduled to give to your Survey of American Law students later in the week. So, rather than completing that exam-writing task you had on your personal docket for the afternoon, you pray you have encouraged your young aspiring human rights advocate and hopefully have offered him some helpful advice. Many of my good and faithful friends back in the States frequently remind me that: "You need to say 'no' more often." And, while I will grant the wisdom of that rebuke when it comes to requests for my participation in administrative task forces, academic committee-work or even some ministry invitations (usually delivered on short-notice), I'm finding that when I seek to be fulfilling the call to teach, I need to be evermore mindful of brother Bonhoeffer's instruction: Allow yourself to be interrupted.

October 31, 2009

Reformation Day

I asked my students here at Handong a question yesterday. What is significant about the date October 31? The Korean Fall Thanksgiving had been celebrated weeks ago. Another festival was soon to come next week, but October 31, what's special about that day? Many of the students had a puzzled look on their faces. I then added to the month and day the year 1517. Now, a few faces brighten! One student spoke softly, "Martin Luther." (That's often the way an answer initially comes, first tentatively and then, after a word of encouragement, with more confidence).

"That's right! What did Luther do on October 31, 1517?" (extended pause) Then a student speaks up, "He nailed that paper to the church door." Correct! And, why did he nail that paper on which he had written those 95 statements, the 95 Theses, to the church door in Wittenburg, Germany? Why would you post a list of thesis statements -- you know what a thesis statement is -- its a statement of your main point -- Why would Luther post a list of 95 statements of truth that he was declaring were very important? Was it so that everyone would read them and take them to be true on their face?"

At this point in the class, some of my more perceptive students were beginning to catch on. They realized that I was giving them an historical example of the foundational practice upon which our classroom lessons and discussion are based. And, while they were not previously aware of the process of calling for a disputation that was the common practice in Luther's day, they surmised that his posting of the 95 Theses was an invitation for others to examine Luther's ideas and to engage in a debate. By posting his 95 Theses, Luther was calling into question the authority of the church to use the practice of purchasing indulgences as a means for obtaining forgiveness of sins as well as challenging many other teachings and practices on the grounds that they were contrary to Holy Scripture. Luther was doing what my students hear as an admonition at the conclusion of each of our class sessions. He was: Questioning everything and seeking to hold on to the good!

7

November 2, 2009

An Occasion to Teach

If you speak English and you are a teacher here in Korea, you will most likely be presented with regular requests to teach those who are interested in learning the language. This is especially true if your aspiring students are children and the one making the request is their parent or, even better, their Sunday School teacher. Such was the case when I was invited a few weeks ago to give a short talk to the "Kids English Bible Study" (KEBS) at The Joyful Church, one of the largest congregations in Pohang. The kids were great, and the teachers were very appreciative of a native English-speaker coming to the class and sharing time with their students.

I was invited back this past Sunday, and have now been asked to give regular (twice-a-month) talks on the Bible lessons the children are studying (Cain and Abel was yesterday morning's story) as well as visit with the small groups of students from 8 to 12 years old, who are more advanced in their English language skills. My experiences teaching the KEBS kids have taken me all the way back to my days as a summer camp counselor and the initial stages of my teaching career that began in a small private elementary school. I'm reminded of those early years when I was first hearing the call and being encouraged by others to teach.

So, whether its in the lecture halls at the university through the week or down in the Bible School classroom on Sunday mornings, I sense a strengthening and renewal of my call each time I'm provided an occasion to teach.

November 10, 2009

Fuji Mountain's Majesty

Over the past five days, I have had the privilege of visiting Japan and attending a wonderful conference for missionaries and church planters. The conference was held at the Fuji Hakone Land Hotel, and this was the view of Mt. Fuji from the conference grounds. I felt beckoned each day to stay outside as I was transfixed by the mountain's majesty.

I was invited to the conference by Laurie Siemers, my good friend and colleague from West Hills, our home church back in St. Louis. The church sends several people to serve with folks from churches in Virginia, Florida and a few other locales who together make-up the U.S. volunteer support team. The team handles the conference logistics as well as putting on a full children's ministry VBS-styled program for the missionary kids. It's a wonderful opportunity to serve those on the mission field and to encourage them in deed and in truth. (1 John 3:18). I met both young and seasoned missionaries from the States. In particular, I was greatly impressed by two young couples who had recently arrived in Japan and are currently in language training school. Their commitment and devotion to God's call upon their lives was a true challenge to my heart.

I also met several missionaries and seminary professors who are Korean and are now serving in Japan. I learned in much more personal ways how God shows the reality of His love to the Japanese people by moving these Korean brothers and sisters to serve them when the history between Japan and Korean has been one filled with evil acts against Korean men, women and children by Japanese soldiers, especially during the period of occupation in the early part of the 20th century. God has enabled many Koreans to love and reach out with forgiveness to those who were once their enemies and oppressors. So while my eyes were filled with the awesomely majestic views of Mt. Fuji and the gloriously gorgeous colors of the autumn landscapes, my heart was even more encouraged by the dedication and devotedness of fellow followers of Christ who have heeded His call upon their lives and are now seeking to respond each day to the challenges of life in a culture that is in many ways is even more individualistic and self-focused than the ways of the West.

I will lift up my eyes unto the hills . . .

November 11, 2009

"You Don't Need a Map When You Have a Guide. . .

. . . The important thing, though, is . . . stay close to your guide." These wise words are from my son, Caleb Andrew. His words resonate with truth not only for outings into the wilderness but also for each day of our lives. As humans, though, we would much rather have a map that lines out for us all the paths lying ahead so that we can be alerted to the challenging roads and be encouraged by knowing our ultimate destination. It's a bit unsettling not to know where you're going and having to rely upon someone else to lead you. But, I was recently reminded while on my journey to Japan that it is indeed much better to have a guide than try to follow a map -- even one with detailed instructions.

I had been given (through a number of emails) wonderfully detailed instructions on how to proceed from Narita International Airport to the adjoining depot to then travel by train via Tokyo Station (the Grand Central of Japan's capital) and a transfer to another train on to Atami Station where I was to look for a bus to the conference center, or should I miss the last bus due to a late arrival, I was then to hail a taxi that would convey me up the narrow, winding mountain road from Atami to the Fuji Hakone Land Hotel. That should have given me confidence. I had the map. My only problem was that I had never been outside of Narita Airport before. My prior travels had only taken me to Japan quick transfers to planes that flew me on destinations beyond in Asia and America. So, even though I had all the information to show how I could get from the airport to the hotel, I had this sinking feeling that my limited ability to take that information and use it in a strange place to find the way would most likely result in my being "a mite bewildered" (since, of course, as an Eagle Scout, I would never get "lost").

To my great relief about two days before I was to travel from Korea to Japan, I received assurance that a dear and faithful sister from Tokyo would plan to meet me upon my arrival at Narita and serve as my guide to get me where I needed to go. It is hard for me to express the peace that flooded my heart and mind when I knew that I would not have to rely upon my own efforts to read and follow a map (and an excellent map at that) but I could rest in the presence of my guide who had promised to be with me along the way. In fact, my guide enabled me to understand the instructions I had been given and encouraged me to ride the express train that was headed for Tokyo Station. I didn't hesitate when she promised to meet me again further down along the way she had set me upon.

Caleb's words had proved true once again. "You don't need a map when you have a guide."

"In paths that they have not known I will guide them. I will turn the darkness before them into light, the rough places into level ground. These are the things I do, and I do not forsake them." (Isaiah 42:16)

November 16, 2009

For Every Sigh there is a Psalm

The Book of Psalms is for many their most favorite book in the Bible. Bonhoeffer wrote from his prison cell, "I love the Psalms. I read them every day." I would have to say that over the years, the Psalms have indeed become my favorite book -- the portion of Scripture that I tend to turn to most often when I seek to pray, when I look for words to express thanksgiving and most especially, when I long to pour out my heart before God.

I cannot now recall where I first read or heard what is, I think, the best seven-word summary of the Psalms, but it often comes to mind, and I've encouraged others in their times of dryness with these words: "For every sigh there is a Psalm." In the Psalms, we meet David in his triumphs and defeats. We read Moses' wisdom and his praise. And, we even hear the hearts of those little known poets of the Lord like Asaph and the sons of Korah.

It should be no surprise then that the words of a Psalm brought with them a refreshing breath of the Spirit to a dry heart. For me, this past weekend, it was Psalm 94:18-19 where the unnamed psalmist writes:

> *I need only say, 'I am slipping,' for your faithful love, Yahweh, to support me; however great the anxiety of my heart, your consolations soothe me.*

His consolations came Sunday morning as I heard an encouraging message emphasizing God's faithfulness to His promise from 2 Samuel 7. In that chapter, God covenants with David, and David's response was simply, "Lord, do as you have said." Later that morning, I gave a talk to the KEBS class at Joyful Church. The lesson assigned to me for the day -- God's promise to Noah, his family and all creatures on the earth that was marked-out by God's setting His bow in the sky. The Lord has His way of reminding us of His care, His promise, His faithfulness that support us however great the anxiety of our hearts or however many the sighs of our souls.

November 17, 2009

"Make This Your Occupation"

"What should my second major be?" This was the question posed by a young man who stopped by my faculty office Monday morning. He is a freshman and a student in my Survey of American Law course. Every student here at Handong is expected to have two majors. Both are to be chosen by the student. My young visitor had already chosen his first major -- U.S. & International Law -- the program of study that I was invited to teach. Now, he was trying to determine his second major. Should it be Informational Technology -- an area in which he has a keen interest; should it be Management & Economics or something else?

How do you go about answering such questions? Some might suggest the "standard" answers: choose a major that will give you a "fall-back" position should your aspirations for law school prove beyond your abilities to achieve. Or, choose a major that will provide you good job opportunities when you graduate. I found myself, though, in a very perplexing spot. I wanted to be helpful and encouraging to my young student. But, I did not want to just give him the "quick answer" he was looking for. Rather, I wanted to challenge and guide him to think for himself.

You see, I'm beginning to learn that most Korean students (and Asian students, in general, for that matter) look to their elders, their professors, their pastors for specific answers. They want to be told what to do; what to think. It is especially true, it appears, in

Korea because of the cultural influence of Confucianism. From my Western perspective, I want to encourage and equip my students to make their own decisions. I don't want to tell them what to think. Instead, I endeavor to train them in how to think clearly, critically and wholly.

I believe my young friend may have been a bit disappointment by the counsel he received from me. I did not give him a simple and direct answer. Rather, I urged him to consider how God has designed and equipped him to serve others. I challenged him to choose a major that would require him to read broadly and write extensively. If he believed that he should pursue the study of law, he would need to develop and hone his analytical thinking and persuasive reasoning skills.

For the follower of Jesus, the most important question is: what is God's call upon my life? This question can be examined by considering the gifts God has given you -- gifts that equip you to serve others. The Apostle Paul wrote you his young protégé, Timothy, *"You have in you a spiritual gift which was given to you . . . Do not neglect it. Let this be your care and your occupation, and everyone will be able to see your progress"* (1 Timothy 4:14-15 NJB).

So your occupation should not be just "your job." We should be occupied -- that is, we should be devoting our time, our energies, and our lives to the manner of serving others that God has equipped us with gifts to perform. In short, we should heed God's calling as our occupation in life. This will transform a student's decision about his major from selecting a course of study that will enable him merely "to make a better living" into choosing a path that will lead him, by God's grace, to "living a better life" by living his life in the service of others.

November 19, 2009

Eating for Pleasure or for Wholeness?

Three of my Korean colleagues took me out for dinner last evening. They assured me that it would be a special treat. The night was cold and blustery. The meal I was promised was especially suited, I was told, to warm chilled bones. The restaurant where we arrived specialized in a traditional Korean "stew." So we sat, traditional Asian-style, cross-legged around a table that rose about 15 inches from the floor. Upon its presentation, the "stew" appeared to be something like a spinach soup. There was a thick body of greens, yet the broth had more than a hint of a seafood flavor. I was later told that the base of the broth was a collection of very small shell fish. My colleagues consumed their bowls of stew with only momentary pauses for conversation. I, on the other hand, was talking more and eating less.

Without a doubt, the substance of the stew was quite healthy and hearty. I'm sure that I would have benefited greatly had I been able to consume more of it. What I found difficult, though, was convincing my taste buds of this truth. It became quite self-evident to me that as a Westerner I have the habit of eating, first and foremost, to please my tongue rather than to fortify my body as a whole. I was, however, able to take a few spoonfuls of rice, submerging them gently into the broth for a moment, and then swallowing quickly before any distinctly Korean flavors had much of an opportunity to stimulate my gustatory faculties. I ingested a small portion of the stew, but I definitely did not savor its flavor.

So, what's this poor American, bound by the habit of eating for pleasure, to do? I ate as much as I could, and then confessed to my brothers that I still have much to learn from them who eat first for the benefit of their whole bodies' health and who have taught their taste buds to appreciate nourishing foods much higher than tantalizing treats. Maybe, that would actually be a very useful approach to all our forms of consumption -- whether it be the food and drink we take-in through our mouths or the images and ideas we "consume" with our eyes and ears. Clearly, Eastern habits of life have much more to teach me.

November 20, 2009

Things We Leave Behind

Discipleship is marked to some measure by things we leave behind. This was clearly true of Jesus' first disciples who left their nets as they responded to his call, "Follow me." A few weeks ago, I engaged in an email correspondence with a good friend and brother on this very subject. The topic has commanded my attention for the better part of the past ten years. I believe, though, that I am just now beginning to be able to articulate what is meant by following Jesus. Here is a portion of what I wrote:

"I have found that the actions that bear witness to true faith and hope are most often actions of the believer giving up, in very practical ways, his life ambitions, possessions, aspirations and desires, and then going where Christ both calls and leads him. So, the more pressing questions of personal examination for me, for you, for any follower of Christ who desires to follow Him in more authentic ways in the here and now, are: What have I given up? Where have I gone? What am I willing to give up? Where am I willing to go?"

"When a person genuinely examines himself/herself with such questions, I would venture to say that for the larger part of the professing church, the answers to what have I given up is very little or nothing, and to where have I gone is for the most part no where. I am thankful that I see in many young people, who today are challenged by the reality of authentic faith and hope, a true willingness and obedience to give up and to go. For in a very real sense, if the answer to the questions of willingness are not "everything" and "anywhere" then we have not truly appreciated what Christ has done for us nor have we begun to enter into what He will do through us." After being here at Handong, though, for the past three months (today marks my 90th day away), I cannot say that I am following Jesus any closer because the authenticity of following is not measured by distance from the things, places or even the people we've left behind. Rather, I believe it can only be evaluated in terms of the nearness of my heart's desire to the person of Christ and the measure to which my volition is filled by the will of God. That desire will often move us to leave things behind, to depart from places of security and to separate, for a time, from even the people that we love more than any other people on earth.

Is this then where we truly find freedom? The kind of freedom Jesus was talking about when he said, "If the Son sets you free, you will be free indeed"? I think it is very much what the Apostle Paul wrote to the Galatians Christians about when he said, "You have been called unto freedom, but do not use your freedom as an occasion for the flesh (i.e. "self-advancement" or "self-gratification"), but by love serve one another. Service of others in the love of Christ will often -- may I say always -- lead us to leave things of our own behind. But it may also call us to depart the familiar places and to separate from people dearly loved.

The problem is, leaving behind, departing and separating are not easy things to do. They don't inspire confidence in our decisions nor a greater sense of commitment to even the noblest cause that may have motivated our actions. Instead, we are often submerged into doubt, but these are the times when we look back not just at what has brought to the place we now find ourselves to be, but also to the paths that others have chosen in their desire to know and do the will of God. In the testimonies of others who have trod upon such pilgrim paths, we find hope and a renewing of our faith in the one whom we follow. We do not walk our journey alone. To follow means we are always walking after another -- the one who has promised to never leave or forsake us. So, may I and you find freedom in the things we leave behind.

> *Truly, truly, I say to you, when you were young, you used to dress yourself and walk wherever you wanted, but when you are old, you will stretch out your hands, and another will dress you and carry you where you do not want to go." (This he said to show by what kind of death he was to glorify God.) And after saying this he said to him, "Follow me."* (John 21:18-19)

November 23, 2009

"I passed along and observed the objects of your worship . . ."

With these words, the Apostle Paul introduced his message to the Stoic and Epicurean philosophers on Mars Hill. Before he attempted to start preaching the Gospel to the people of Athens, Paul had taken time to walk around and carefully observe their culture, their religious practices and their ways of living life. Every culture, every place has objects of worship. For Korea, Buddhism has had a substantial impact upon the formation of its culture. This past Saturday, I was invited to travel to Gyeongju, the ancient capital city of Korea, and to tour Bulguksa Temple by my good friend and young brother, Kris and his wife Mary, who is a 3d year law student soon to graduate from Handong International Law School.

In many ways, Gyeongju is the Athens of Korea. As we stepped through Bulguksa's gates, we began to realize that we were entering a very special place. Bulguksa is known as "Buddha's country temple." Within the monastery are two of the oldest pagodas in Korea. They are among the country's national treasures. While we were passing along through the temple grounds, we observed both the objects of worship and their worshippers. We met one elderly Korean lady who serves within the temple (most likely an "Anna" of this temple) and, though, we could not communicate with her in words, she was drawn to Kris and Mary's little 18 month-old daughter, Sadie Rose. She displayed the warmth and tenderness of a grand mother, and her face glowed when Sadie Rose gave her a smile.

I wonder if what I sensed as we made our way around the temple and its cloister walk was something like what Paul experienced as he perused the Athenian altars. Just as the Apostle heard echoes of God's truth in the words of the Greek poets and philosophers (see Acts 17:26-28), I perceived the wisdom of the ages in several decorative scrolls upon which monks from the temple had written some sayings of the Buddha. One read, "Go on your way with one mind." It prompted me to think of the admonition in James 1 to single-minded devotion to Christ. Another said, "The fragrance of a flower may last for 1,000 miles, but the aroma of a virtuous life will endure for 10,000 years." That one reminded me of Paul's description of followers of Jesus as an "aroma of Christ" in 2 Corinthians 2. Kris and I talked as we walked about the ways we can see God's common grace reaching out and speaking to and through diverse cultures.

It takes time to "observe the objects of worship" in other cultures. I'm sure Paul spent several days walking about Athens before he found the altar to the "Unknown God." That altar became his entree to conversation with the people who spent there days hanging out on Mars Hills discussing the latest ideas of the day. I don't think I'll encounter any Stoics or Epicureans around these parts, but maybe a deeper appreciation of the sayings of the Buddha may equip me to engage one of his followers who are without a doubt are -- like those in the Athens of Paul's day -- a very religious people.

November 26, 2009

He Who Would Be Great, Must Be . . .

. . . the servant of all. Jesus embodied this truth throughout his life and especially in his death. He also said, "I did not come to be served, but to serve and to give my life as a ransom for all." This way of living, though, goes completely against the grain of human nature. Our natural inclination is to be served, to be preferred over others, and above all, to be first. What I am learning during my time here is that human nature is basically the same in any culture, and the way of life shown to us by Jesus is counter-cultural no matter where you are on earth.

This realization came home to me a couple of evenings ago when I decided to head over to Hyoam Restaurant -- the best place to eat on campus -- for my dinner. It's a popular spot among both students and faculty. When I arrived, the line was quite long, so I took up my place at the end and waited. The special on Tuesday evenings is breaded pork tenderloin. It tends to be one of the hottest sellers. As I waited for the line to progress toward the front counter where orders are placed, I was hoping (okay, I was also praying) that there would be at least one pork tenderloin left.

When I had made it about half-way up to the counter, I noticed that someone was quickly moving up the line, passing by me and going straight to the front. Hold-on a second! I've been waiting in this line for nearly 10 minutes, patiently taking gradual steps along the way as I watched more and more people ahead of me walk away with their trays filled with the pork tenderloin special. Who was this guy cutting-in line? Only later did I learn (after the special sold-out and I ended up with the "not-so teriyaki" chicken) that he was a faculty member. Evidently, the custom on campus allows faculty members to go to the head of the line. They need not wait their turn with everyone else. That's the local practice.

I thought about that for a while. I had every right in this culture to go straight to the front of the line, and no one would object. But then, I reflected. What would be better for a teacher to do? One who is attempting to teach in the classroom about living like a follower of Christ in every dimension life? Would it be better to prefer myself or to defer and wait my turn in line like all the students? So now, I run the risk of acting in a manner not expected of faculty on this campus if I simply wait my turn in line for a meal. I'm finding, though, that being "counter-cultural" is our calling when it comes to the commands of Christ. Jesus took time on the night he was betrayed not only to share a last supper with his disciples, but also to wash their feet. He calls us to follow him -- to love others just as he has loved us -- to take up the basin and the towel.

> *Love one another with brotherly affection. Outdo one another in showing honor. Do not be slothful in zeal, be fervent in spirit, serve the Lord.* (Romans 12:10-11)

November 27, 2009

Thanksgiving Half-a-World Away

Although this is the first Thanksgiving I have ever experienced apart from my family, I've been sustained by the fellowship of new friends, and I've been reminded of the blessings that are bestowed upon us through our brothers and sisters in the body of Christ. I'm also thankful for the blessing of internet technology that enabled me to enjoy a video call with my family who had gathered at my mother's home for a traditional Thanksgiving feast. In spite of the fact that I'm half-a-world away from the people I love the most, I was enabled to give thanks this year in ways more meaningful to me than ever before.

Give thanks to the Lord, for he is good,
for his steadfast love endures forever.

It is he who remembered us in our low estate,
for his steadfast love endures forever;

And rescued us from our foes,
for his steadfast love endures forever;

He who gives food to all flesh,
for his steadfast love endures forever.

Give thanks to the God of heaven,
for his steadfast love endures forever.

(Psalm 136:1,23-26)

November 28, 2009

You're No Song and Dance Man!

Have I mentioned just how much Korean students love to sing and dance? Not just the drum and cymbal corps (who, by the way, are still banging away these nights), but virtually every Korean student I've met is quite the singer and almost as many are dancers, or at least they don't hesitate to try to be dancers. So, it should come as no surprise that my students have been appealing to me to participate (I used that word advisedly; note, I did not say "perform") in their various talent contests over these past few weeks. Or, maybe that is a surprise, or at least should be -- since I've never been known as a dancer (maybe a shuffler, at most) and my singing is best kept within the confines of a large choir. A couple of Friday nights ago, I was recruited into serving as one of several judges for an "open-mic" evening at the "I-Cafe" (that's the International Cafe that operates within the Student Union especially for those members of the Handong student body who are from countries other than Korea). There were singers from Mongolia, Thailand, Cambodia, Korea, and the U.S., dancers from the Democratic Republic of Congo, Haiti and Russia, a linguist from Afghanistan (who could translate any phrase posed to him into 8 languages) and even a would-be comedian from the State of Washington (an exchange student from La Tourneau University). To top it all off, the emcee was from Tajikistan. The winners, though, were all singers: third place to a young man from Korea, second to a young lady from Russia, and first to a young man from the States who played the guitar and sang with echoes of Eric Clapton. Well, serving as a judge for the I-Cafe open-mic night was only my initiation into the world of student talent at Handong. The following week, I began rehearsing with a group of Korean law students for the annual "Battle of the Schools" talent contest where each school within the university presents a singing and dancing troupe in performance on center stage, under the lights, and on camera.

The first number our group was to perform was a four-part choral arrangement of St. Francis' Prayer for Peace -- in Korean! Thankfully, I was placed along side a young man with a strong and resonant bass voice, so following the music was rendered much easier. My challenge, however, was to get close enough to a correct pronunciation of the Korean words so that my trembling bass voice did not sound out when it should have been silent. All and all, though, the singing was a breeze compared to what lay ahead of me in the second half of our performance. Our second number was a dance routine, though, not a thoughtful, slow-paced waltz. That would have been much more my speed, but oh no! These Korean kids love to jump and kick and spin and even shake their hips and heads, at the same time! In a very smart move on our dance director's part (after she had witnessed my first feeble attempts during the initial rehearsals of the routine), I was placed in the third row center, surrounded by young students who had mastered every move. I really have no idea how I did. It was fun, but exhausting. We were the seventh group to go on that evening, and I think we made it to the stage around 10pm. I'm told the whole thing was video-taped, but you can be sure that if it was, that video will never see the light of day (at least I hope it never will). I do remember the last move of our routine -- a coordinated salute that I'm fairly sure I managed with my right hand and on the final beat. If the performance is ever viewed again, then whoever sees it will conclude with me that I'm definitely NO song and dance man!

November 29, 2009

Why I Teach

A week or so ago, I received an email from Mark Johnson, the Director of Public Relations at Fontbonne University. It was an email that he had sent out to all Fontbonne faculties. Mark asked a simple question: "Why do you teach?" Here's my answer to his question ~ All of us teach others through what we say, how we act and the ways in which we live each day. Whether we intend to or not, we are influencing, instructing and, in many ways, shaping the lives of others. A few people are privileged and enabled to be involved in this endeavor in a purposeful way. I teach because I've been shaped and equipped by others to teach, and when I'm teaching I sense that I'm being the person and doing the very human activity I was designed to be and equipped to do. I been given the opportunity to teach at several different institutions during my career, and I can say without the slightest hesitation that my experiences teaching at Fontbonne have been the most enriching. Here I've been encouraged and supported to create learning experiences together with my students that flow out of pondering the questions of life. Questions like those posed by Neil Postman and Charles Weingartner in their book, **Teaching as a Subversive Activity:** "What, if anything, seems to you to be worth dying for? What seems worth living for? How can 'good' be distinguished from 'evil'?" Equipping and challenging others to reflect upon these sorts of questions is, to me, what teaching is all about. ~ I wrote those words as I reflected upon my teaching experiences the past four years at Fontbonne in St. Louis. During these past four months teaching here at Handong, I continue to sense a renewal of my calling to teach. The renewal comes through an on-going openness to ask myself those persistent questions and to listen to others for insights into their answers.

8

December 3, 2009

To Question or Not to Question? . . . That is the Question!

As a teacher, I have been endeavoring over the past four months here at Handong both to encourage and to challenge my students to ask questions. My approach, though, runs contrary to the inclination not to question that most Asian students have had instilled within them from their culture (or at least, that's the explanation that is most often offered to me for their hesitation, and in some cases, out-right resistance to raising questions). Many view questioning not as a positive expression of desire for deeper understanding of an idea, but rather as a negative attack that seeks to undermine the "authority" of the teacher as well as create divisions and doubt. From this perspective, listening quietly is expected of students, rather than questioning openly. There are, though, some questions that are not aimed at understanding. In my reading, I recently encountered Paul's admonition to avoid *"foolish and undisciplined speculations, understanding that they only give rise to quarrels"* (2 Timothy 2:23).

So, if there are some questions that are either motivated by or are aimed at creating quarrels, for the sake of quarreling, then we would have to acknowledge that not all questions are of equal value. Not every question should be entertained. Not every question should even be aired. Some questions are constructive.

They lead toward building understanding and strengthening learning relationships. But other questions may be corrupting. These sorts of questions are intended to foster greater misunderstanding and confusion. The problem is, however, that any given question on its face may not reveal its true character; or, should I say, the question itself may not disclose the true character and intentions of the one who poses the question. Since we are all humans who are engaged in the endeavor of education, I must ever be on guard that the questions I put to others be questions truly seeking understanding and not be questions meant to divide, harm others, and corrupt the pursuit of truth for the sake of self-justification.

All of these thoughts came to bear upon me yesterday, when I pondered whether I should raise a question in response to a guest speaker's presentation that was, as I pondered, being delivered to our faculty. The presenter was a former Egyptian Muslim imam who had converted to Christianity. He now gives presentations to governmental organizations as well as educational institutions and private groups around the world. He had, in fact, just before arriving in Korea been in Switzerland where he consulted with several members of the government there. In his presentation, the speaker set forth twenty-two of the thirty articles in the Universal Declaration of Human Rights adopted by the member countries of the United Nations in 1948 and compared various selections from the Islamic Scriptures to each of these articles in his effort to demonstrate that the teachings and practices of the Muslim religion violate the UN Declaration. He then argued that action against the spread of Islam should be taken by those nations that recognize the Declaration as a standard for human rights.

He gave as his one and only example of the type of action for which he was calling the recent adoption by the Swiss people of a ban on the construction of minarets at mosques within Switzerland. What the speaker, however, failed to acknowledge in his presentation was that the Swiss action banning the construction of minarets was in and of itself a violation of the provision of the UN Declaration which expressly acknowledges that: "Everyone has the right to freedom of thought, conscience and religion; this right includes freedom to change his religion or belief, and freedom, either alone or in community with others and in public or private, to manifest his religion or belief in teaching, practice, worship and observance" (*emphasis added*). As I sat and listened to the speaker's presentation, I began to formulate several questions to pose to our guest should the audience be given that opportunity. My questions were: "Do you believe that the UN Declaration is a standard for human rights that all countries should follow? If so (and I assumed that the speaker would say yes to my first question) have you considered whether the Swiss ban on minarets is an action that itself violates the UN Declaration?"

I must readily admit that I wished to expose the evident inconsistency in the speaker's presentation with much more directness and force. No public Q&A time was offered, though, and when I went up to talk with the speaker personally his limited time was occupied by many who were approving of his comments. I did, however, raise my concerns with a few fellow faculty members who were also waiting to talk with our guest speaker. So, I didn't put my questions to the speaker. This morning I found an interesting article by Dr. Albert Mohler commenting on the Swiss banning of minarets. I emailed this article out to all of my fellow faculty members here at Handong and promptly received several replies that indicated I was not the only one who was raising questions about what we had heard. One colleague wrote: "read [Mohler's article] with interest. Thanks much. Certainly consistent with what you were suggesting yesterday." While I must be on guard not to use questions improperly, it is better to question than not to question. All ideas, all opinions, all things need to be examined by questions.

December 5, 2009

Having Ears You Do Not Hear

When you are an alien living as stranger in a strange land, you tend to associate your new experiences with ones you've had before. You do this to try to better understand your past, the present and how you might make your way through the days that lie ahead of you. This week, I realized that my current experiences can deepened my appreciation of others I've come to know in the past. One of the most interesting experiences in my past has been the opportunity I've been given to learn from those who are deaf. Over the last 15 years, I've come to understand the Deaf culture better through spending time with them. My wife is a sign-language interpreter, among many other things, and together with her I've met and become good friends with many Deaf, and through my wife's assistance, I've learned much from them.

I recall vividly my first real insight into Deaf culture. It came through a story teller who explained the drastically different reactions he received when as a young boy he had been taught to voice words. When he attempted to voice the simple sentence "I like baseball," those who heard his halting expressions of sounds reacted as if, according to his account, he was mentally impaired. When, however, later in this story teller's life, he entered into groups of hearing people and began to express himself with sign language, the reactions he received showed that those who observed his signing acknowledged him to be a very intelligent person. They realized that he knew a language that they did not know.

For the first time, I realized that signing is a distinct language in itself, and those who use it to communicate are just like any other person who might speak German, French or even Korean. I realized that a person's intelligence is not impaired by a disability, but rather their intelligence is demonstrated by their ability to overcome a perceived limitation through new forms of communication. Now, for me here in Korea, amongst a majority of people whose language I do not understand nor speak (and have to this point made very little progress in learning), I am the one with the disability. I am the one at the disadvantage. And just this past Thursday evening, it finally dawned upon me that I am the one who, in a certain, small way, is deaf in this culture. I hear sounds but I understand nothing or nearly nothing.

Thursday evening was the annual university Christmas concert. While some of the songs where performed in English, all of the spoken introductions and explanations were in Korean. I thought to myself, "I'm sure those who organized this concert realized that at least a few people in the audience would not be Korean-speakers. Why didn't they provide a translator?" When teaching in the States at Fontbonne University, I noted that every university event provided sign-language interpretation. This is most likely because Fontbonne is known for its outstanding Deaf Education department and often deaf or hearing-impaired are among those attending the events. The University consciously seeks to provide the means for communicating understanding to all who attend.

So, as I sat there at the Christmas concert and listened to the emcee introduce acts and to performers explaining whatever it was they were explaining, I acquired a deeper understanding of what it means to have ears but still not hear. But if that is all I learned, I'm not listening very well. My failure to hear, to understand cannot be blamed on the failure or deficiency of others. I bear the responsibility for seeking to understand. I may not now have the ability, in and of myself, to gain the understanding, but I bear the responsibility to ask for it. No one is alone sufficient to achieve understanding. We will always need others. Though I have ears, I always need others to help me hear.

December 9, 2009

Sitting Down to Dine

This past Friday evening I had the privilege of being invited to the "End of Semester Party" put on by our International Student Union here at Handong. This is the same group that hosted the "open mic" night a few weeks back where I was asked to serve as one of the competition's judges. The invitation came by text message to my mobile. I was further advised that a car would come by to pick me up and transport me to the party venue. In many respects, I felt as if I were being given the VIP treatment. The evening's festivities did not disappoint in any regard. If fact, the whole experience reflected all of the many and varied dimensions of the cross-cultural engagements I have been provided during my first four months of teaching here. The banquet afforded both traditional Korean dishes as well as a wide selection of entrées from throughout Asia and even a few Western-styled items. Needless to say, we were more than abundantly provided for.

But what was an even a greater blessing, though, was the delight and true joy I experienced from the fellowship of sitting around a table with students from eleven different countries, including Haiti, Congo, Cameroon, Tanzania, Ethiopia, Afghanistan, Tajikistan, Russia, Mongolia, China, and India. In addition, there were also students from Kenya, Thailand, Philippines and Korea. Nearly all the students joined in both singing and dancing to traditional songs from their home countries. It was one of those evenings that you wish would continue on for hours more. As I read the Scriptures these days, the phrase "all nations" has begun to stand out in new ways. I sense that I am being given a small preview of the glorious gathering that awaits us when people from every tribe, language, and nation will join together in unity around the throne of God.

December 11, 2009

The Ministry of Bearing

As I'm coming to the close of my first four months in Korea, I have been experiencing this past week what some of my American colleagues tell me is a common disposition in first-time foreigners. In spite of all the wonderful opportunities to celebrate the accomplishments of students at the end of the academic year, I have been thinking and acting a whole lot more like Scrooge than Santa Claus – no matter how hard I've tried to work-up a holiday spirit. Nearly every little thing throughout each day that otherwise might only be a minor irritant has now, from my perspective, transformed into a major -- did I say MAJOR -- source of consternation!!!!! My patience is wearing thinner and thinner. (For my regular readers, you may have noticed a shift in tone in some of my recent posts).

I am so ready to get back to the States for what I'm looking forward to -- a few wonderful weeks of renewed fellowship with my dearly loved ones. My only consolation, at this point, is to confess my failures to love and bear with my new brothers and sisters, and trust the forgiving grace of our Lord. I have been reminded of my deep need to ask God to cultivate within me a servant's heart. Brother Bonhoeffer teaches us to serve one another in very practical ways. One of the chief means of service is what he describes as the ministry of bearing. As followers of Christ we are called upon to bear the burdens of others.

Those burdens include the other "person's nature, individuality, endowment. It also includes his weaknesses and oddities, which are such a trial to our patience, everything that produces frictions, conflicts, and collisions among us." "To bear the burden of the other person means involvement with the created reality of the other, to accept and affirm it, and, in bearing with it, to break through to the point where we take joy in it." (Life Together, 101). I have not yet made that break through to joy. I know that I am not capable of it. So, if it should occur (and only the others with whom I am called to bear will know for sure) it will only occur by the grace and mercy of Christ.

December 12, 2009

As the World Sleeps . . .

Asia rises! Those are the words I hear each morning when I turn on Channel NewsAsia to catch-up on the latest events impacting our lives in today's global society. And, it's true! As my family and friends back in the States settle in for a night of rest, we here in Asia have already arisen from our beds (or for the more authentic Asians, from their mats) and have begun the next new day.

But that statement is much more than a comment on the difference in time zones between the Western Hemisphere and the East. In many real and practical ways, Asia is rising to greater and greater prominence on the world stage while a good deal of the rest of the world is sleeping, or at least slogging along. The ascendance of China and India to the status of leading nations in the global economy is as indisputable as it is inevitable in light of the current trends in both the West and the East.

So what's to be made of Asia's rising? Are we to perceive it as a threat or is it the marker of movement for the 21st century? The sun never sat on Britannia in the 19th century, and near the close of the 20th, America claimed sole possession of dominance among world powers after the fall of the Soviet Union. But today, if we are honest with ourselves, we must admit that the status of the United States as foremost leader in the arenas of power – economic and military – has been and continues to decline, while the increasing emergence of Asian countries into prominent roles in global affairs is being recognized by every leader of the West.

The community of humanity will always consist of differing peoples, tribes, languages and nations. Rather than angling for positions of control, power and prestige, maybe it is time for us to learn to bow a bit more often and even a bit deeper.

> *God opposes the proud, but gives grace to the humble . . . . Draw near to God, and he will draw near to you. Cleanse your hands, you sinners, and purify your hearts, you double-minded.* (James 4:6-8)

December 18, 2009

So Just What is a Global University?

Today marks the conclusion of my first semester of teaching at Handong Global University. My students completed their final exams in each of my three courses over the past two days. Now, I have only to finish marking them and then to submit the final grades each has earned. Here at the end of the fall term, I find myself pondering a question that has been presenting itself to me for some time now. What is it about Handong that makes it a "global" university? There are many "state" universities, quite a few "national" ones (Seoul National, just to name one) and even several "international" universities around the world. But just what is a "global" university?

Though it may not be apart of the university's name, there is hardly any institution of higher education these days that doesn't say that it is challenging and equipping its students to think and act globally. When communication can be accomplished at the speed of the Internet and transportation to nearly any location on six continents (I'm excluding Antarctica at this point, though I'm sure a few airlines will start making regular commercial flights there and back any day now) takes merely hours rather than days, weeks or months, this world has become in many respects a global community. But what do we mean when we say we are seeking to think and to act globally? What's more, how might I help others to begin to think and act in this way? How might the members of a university -- as a community of thinking, learning and doing -- authentically embody the idea of being global? I'm sure there are some who have begun to engage this question in thoughtful ways. My experience here over the past four months leads me to conclude that a part of the beginning of being a global university is found in students and faculty who are already living their lives for others.

I have found it in students who have come to this university wishing to be further formed and equipped to serve the needs of others wherever they might be called to serve. For most, this means looking ahead to serving back in their home countries -- serving for the greater good of developing their home countries. For some, it means being willing to go to any of the emerging countries in order to assist them in their development through the rule of law and the upholding of human rights. These two young men are great examples of the students I'm describing. Prophete, from Haiti is studying international law, and Edward, from Tanzania, is studying management and economics. Both demonstrate exceptional servant leadership qualities. Both are planning to return to their home countries after completing their studies. Both have taught me more of what it means to be apart of a global university.

I don't know that anyone here would say that Handong has a corner on the "global" idea of a university, but in some very significant ways the students and faculty are living it out as they seek to live more deliberately and unreservedly for others here, at home or wherever they may be called to serve.

Second Year

9

February 15, 2010

A Walking-Paced Life

Greetings once again from Pohang, Korea! My wife and I have just arrived back on Handong's campus after nearly 20 hours of traveling. The new spring term is shortly to begin and so we're embarking on the next stage of our sojourn here. Over the past seven weeks of winter break, I enjoyed a wonderful time of refreshment visiting with family and friends in St. Louis and Portland. Something dawned upon me, though, within my first few days back in the States -- the pace of life in the U.S. is substantially faster than the pace I had been experiencing here at Handong over the fall term. This realization came during my second week back in St. Louis as I was driving along Interstate 44 (at the speed limit) from downtown, where I had attended the Urbana Missions Conference at the A.G. Edwards Dome, out to Fenton. I started to become quite aware that my days back home had been very stressful and tense. I thought that I would have been relieved to be in familiar surroundings, but I was experiencing quite the opposite -- greater tension, increased stressfulness.

Then, like the proverbial light bulb going off over my head, it came to me. For over four months while living in Korea, I had been leading a walking-paced life on the campus of Handong. I lived where I taught, where I worshipped, even where I shopped and occasionally went out to eat (at Mom's Kitchen -- a favorite little restaurant in the Student Union). As I was back in St. Louis, however, all I had been doing was driving every day. You had to drive to get anywhere you needed to go in nearly every case. What a difference! -- A driving-paced life on the one hand and a walking-paced life on the other. It doesn't take a great deal of analysis to conclude which pattern of living is more favorable to a happy and healthy emotional, intellectual and spiritual life. So, now that we are back in Korea and back to living on Handong's campus, we are looking forward to getting back into a walking-pace of life. I find it quite interesting that the life of one who lives by and through the gracious gift of God in Christ is described by the Apostle Paul as a "walk" and not a "run". With this awareness, Rich Mullins wrote: "Step by step you lead me and I will follow you all of my days."

If we live by the Spirit, let us also walk by the Spirit.
(Galatians 5:25)

February 16, 2010

Happy Lunar New Year!

Our first full day here at Handong is actually the first day of the New Year on the Chinese calendar. February 15 marks the beginning of The Year of the Tiger. It seems appropriate that this day mark a new beginning for us. As I look back now, I'm realizing that my first semester was a time of preparation. This semester will be a time of challenge, no doubt, but I trust that it will also be a time of formation and growth both for Sandy and me personally and for us together in our relationship now in our 31st year of marriage. We'll need to take each day step-by-step -- at a walking pace. Today we walked over to view the new apartment that had been assigned to us only to find that it had several issues that will prevent us moving in. We're making the most of my old studio apartment here in the Mission House where I lived last term. It actually is quite adequate for us. Sandy even referred to the old apartment as my "tent" since it is just a bit bigger in space than a large family tent we borrowed and used many years ago on one of our family vacations with the kids in Colorado. Sandy has made the most of the limited cooking facilities and has already prepared a wonderful spaghetti dinner and an evening meal of pork mandu and vegetables. I definitely won't go hungry this semester and it's very likely that I won't be losing any weight even though I could stand to. All in all, it looks like this New Year has begun well. We'll be trusting the Lord for grace each day as it progresses in these coming months.

February 17, 2010

You Shall Live in Tents

About twelve years ago, when Sandy and I and the kids were moving from a 2,900 sq. ft., two-story colonial (that we had built when I thought I was on my way to becoming a partner at a large law firm) to a 950 sq. ft. ranch walkout in a much older section of Fenton, I began to say -- in a good humored-way -- that I was working my way toward living in a tent. I had left my law practice and had been involved in ministry with a young, small church while also beginning to teach part-time at Missouri Baptist (then) College. Down-sizing came with the territory.

I would joke with the family that "tent-living" was much more in keeping with the pattern of life described in the Bible, but only Caleb and Hannah thought that it sounded like I had a good plan. Well, it seems that the Lord also has a sense of humor. He's brought my "aspiration" to fruition in a way I did not anticipate. It appears that we'll be staying here in what I had referred to last semester as my "hermitage" -- the very small but very adequately appointed studio apartment in the Mission House. (That's our front door on the first level; I took this picture last August when I first moved-in; those rocks in the front are all covered with snow right now). It is, however, no longer a hermitage. Now, it has come to be called our "tent." It's working-out pretty well, though. We do have a wonderful scenic view of pine-covered rolling hills out the back through a window that stretches across nearly the entire length of the rear wall of our laundry and storage room with sliding glass floor to ceiling doors separating the laundry room from our studio. Sandy loves the natural light and the fact that we don't have to climb three flights of stairs with groceries and laundry (the other apartment would have been on the 3d floor of another building). We've also been promised a second wardrobe which, when it is delivered, will provide sufficient space for all our clothes. Other than that, and the fact that none of the apartments on campus have ovens (evidently the Koreans do not do any baking; instead, just steaming, boiling and frying on stove-tops), we pretty much have what is needed to live comfortably. The studio is, to say the least, close quarters, but hey, aren't you supposed to grow closer and closer over 31 years of marriage! We are in a land of sojourning here, and tent-living is beginning to suit us fine for the time.

> *You shall not build a house; you shall not sow seed; you shall not plant or have a vineyard; but you shall live in tents all your days, that you may live many days in the land where you sojourn.* (Jeremiah 35:7)

February 20, 2010

Staying Up Late and Rising Early

Our first week back at Handong has been filled with a variety of meetings and tasks aimed at orienting the faculty to a new academic year and instilling us with a renewed sense of vision and purpose in our callings to learn and teach others. Each day has been filled with sessions where the speakers have found some interesting ways to extend their presentations well beyond the time allotted on the published schedule of events for the faculty retreat. One speaker, in particular, announced at the beginning of his lecture that he would require three hours to make his speech even though he had been slated for only one. As he neared the 90-minute mark, he was handed a note informing him of the need to conclude so that he would be able to catch his flight back to Seoul. Instead of bringing his remarks to a prompt conclusion, he publicly requested the University's president to change his flight schedule so that he might have sufficient time to complete his presentation.

What's even more challenging than late-night meetings, though, is an expectation that you should also be able to rise up early each morning for a time of personal devotion and community prayer. Now, I'll acknowledge that early rising is both a good habit and one that is modeled by many throughout the Scriptures. Bonhoeffer makes a succinct case for this discipline in Life Together. On the other hand, there is explicit guidance in the Word against attempting to combine the two -- staying up late and rising early. So, while adjusting to a new culture is clearly a challenge, maintaining and cultivating a healthy and balanced pattern of life is paramount, wherever you may be living and whatever the expectations of others may be upon your life.

> *It is in vain that you rise up early and go late to rest, eating the bread of anxious toil; for he gives to his beloved sleep.* (Psalm 127:2)

February 23, 2010

Commencement @ the Commencement of the New Year

This past Saturday, Handong Global University convened its 12th Commencement Exercises. Throughout my teaching experience in the States, university commencement ceremonies were traditionally held at the end of the academic year. You would often hear speakers making the comment that though the ceremony occurred at the end of the academic year, it is called "Commencement" because it marks the beginning of a new stage in the life of each graduate. The Asian tradition, however, places the graduation ceremony at the beginning of the academic year, and I think they get it right. Not only does Commencement mark a new start for the many students who are graduating, it also signals a new beginning for the entire university community. It was a joy to see several of my students, who I had had the privilege of teaching in the past fall term, step up to the platform as their names were announced.

Another excellent tradition is practiced by the faculty at Commencement here at Handong. The graduates are called up to the dais according to their schools. For example, all of the graduates from the School of Management and Economics are called forward and their names are read. Next, all the graduates from the School of Life Sciences are called forward. Later, the graduates from the School of Law, where I teach, are also called forward. As each school's graduates are announced, the faculty from that school lines up across the platform. Groups of graduates step up in a line stretching across the dais with a student standing in front of each faculty member. The student bows to the professor and the professor then takes the tassel that hangs from the student's mortar board and moves it from the right side to the left side thus marking, by this symbolic gesture, the student's passing to the graduated status. The professor then congratulates the graduate with a hardy hand-shake and often, in this culture, a hug.

As the New Year here in Asia has recently been celebrated, it was a genuine pleasure to participate in Handong's 12th Commencement Ceremony at this the commencement of the new academic term!

February 24, 2010

The Gift of Mercy

My wife never ceases to amaze me. She's been here on this new continent, in this new country, among a completely new and different culture for only one week, and yet she still has such a sensitivity to the needs of others as well as the personal initiative to get done what needs to get done, especially when it comes to helping another person -- whose name she doesn't even know -- obtain some measure of relief from physical pain. Sandy demonstrated yet again --even here in this totally new environment -- that she has the gift of mercy.

It all took place Sunday morning. We had been picked-up by Prof. Rhee who not only teaches in the Graduate School of Education at Handong but also serves as a teacher and leader for the Kids English Bible Study (KEBS) at Joyful Church in downtown Pohang. I had been invited last semester to present the English Bible Story lessons at KEBS, and this semester the church leaders have asked both Sandy and me to serve as helpers and teachers for the kids on a regular basis. Sunday was the KEBS orientation. Over 75 children, ages 8 to 12, have been enrolled by their parents in the class. The class is aimed at providing a double benefit -- instruction in God's Word, first and foremost, and also English language instruction. Each of the teachers introduced himself or herself to the other members of the KEBS leadership team.

There will be 16 teachers who will handle small groups of the children. Sandy introduced herself briefly, but I followed-up and informed the leadership team that Sandy was not only an experienced Sunday School teacher, she was also a Physical Therapist Assistant and a nursing student as well as a former administrative assistant to the Provost of a university in the States.

One of the other Korean teachers introduced herself but apologized for not standing-up due to back pain that she was experiencing. Following the introductions, Sandy went to this young lady and began to assess her pain and offer some help. As Sandy was assisting her in walking up a flight of stairs, she realized that the young lady was in severe pain and needed to get home and lie down to rest. The young lady, however, had driven herself to church. She was now in no condition to drive due to the pain in her back. Sandy came back down to the Sunday School room and asked Mr. Kim, one of the Korean men on the leadership team who spoke English quite well, to drive along with us while we took the young lady back to her apartment. He drove his car so that Sandy and I would have a ride back to the church. And who might you suspect was going to drive the young lady's car through the busy traffic of downtown Pohang on an early Sunday afternoon? That would be me. Sandy was in the back seat attending to the young lady in pain.

Well, I managed to find my way to her apartment without running any red lights or missing any turns. (Actually, it was a pretty straight shot down one major street after I successfully navigated my way through the packed church parking lot). The young lady lived with her parents in one of the typical high-rise Korean apartments. I was even able to find an open parking place near the young lady's building. Sandy walked her in and took her up to the apartment assuring that she was safely entrusted to the care of her parents. As I observed Sandy caring for this young lady in pain, I once again realized how naturally grace and mercy flow through her to serve the needs of others. One with the gift of mercy serves whenever and wherever she senses the needs of others -- whether in St. Louis, Missouri among her children, grand children, friends and church family or in Pohang, Korea among people whose names she does not yet even know.

10

March 2, 2010

First Day's Daunting

The first day of the new term can be daunting. When you look at your first class roster and see more names than the number of seats in the classroom you've been assigned, you can feel a bit overwhelmed. But, with the help of your able Teaching Assistant, you scout out available, larger classrooms down the hall and find, to your great relief, that the largest lecture room in the new wing of your building is open and accommodates all of the students who have registered for your course -- even the ones on the waiting list who are making heart-felt appeals for admission.

As the room begins to fill, you are pleased to see that you actually recognize some of the students as those who had taken (and survived) one of your classes in the past fall term. You think to yourself, "Maybe this term I'll even be able to master some of their names." Then, it happens. More students arrive. Now there are students who are on neither the class roster nor the waiting list! That daunting feeling begins to creep up on you again. As the seats begin to fill, the students are thankful that you have selected the largest classroom, but you begin to suspect that a more moderate-sized one might have been a better choice. The time comes to begin your introduction and overview of the course, and after a few words of personal greeting, you invite each of the students to introduce himself and herself. As each rises to do so, up and down through all of the many rows, you realize once again why you do what you do. Each face is full of expression. Each voice speaks with its own accent -- Korean, both South and North, Vietnamese, Tajik and Mongolian as well as a few Korean Americans who grew up in Minnesota, New Jersey or California, and even other Koreans who have lived in South Africa and Senegal. You have been given the opportunity of leading and the privilege of learning together with some of the best and brightest students from around the world. While the day began under daunting circumstances, by the end of the first class period that overwhelming feeling has transformed into an enveloping excitement. The new term has begun. Its time to seize the day, and undertake another journey with your students as together you continue to pose and ponder the persistent questions of life.

Test everything; hold fast what is good. (1 Thessalonians 5:21)

March 9, 2010

Lifelong Learning in Balance

Balance is one of the essential keys to living wholly. The Greeks taught moderation in all things -- the golden mean. The Scriptures, too, teach balance -- particularly in the arena of study. On the one hand, Paul exhorts Timothy to "study to show himself approved unto God as servant of the truth who is able to "cut a straight line" with God's Word. (See 2 Timothy 2:15). On the other hand, though, Solomon warns us that "there is no end" to the "making of many books," and "much study is weariness to the flesh." (Ecclesiastes 12:12). Hence, balance is also the key to study. When, however, you live on a university campus just a short walk from your office and two libraries, not to mention having ready access in both home and office, via the Internet, to a wide array of library collections from institutions of higher learning around the world, you are daily confronted with the temptation to live an unbalanced life -- to engage in "much study" and aspire to the "making of many books." A life lived according to the golden mean easily escapes you. A life of balance can be an even greater challenge, though, in the face of requests for your assistance with the learning of others. In the past week, I have been approached by three different people asking for my help with the forming and leading of study groups (both a law student group and a faculty group) and the mentoring of other faculty. My first inclination is to offer whatever help I may be able to give. Jesus' words, "Freely you have received, freely give" come to mind. I want to encourage others in their desire to learn and grow in knowledge as well as in faith.

So what's a person, who believes they have been called to teach, to do? The Chinese proverb written along the side of this post says: "Study is eternal." That is, the pursuit of truth, insight and understanding is a lifelong endeavor. Each day we're on the path of learning. Our progress along the way, though, will be substantially enhanced by keeping our life, as a whole, in balance. Even as we seek to respond to the requests and inquiries of others, we must maintain a balance in our life together of learning. Bonhoeffer suggests in Life Together that one of the key means of maintaining balance in life is to live each day as both a day with others and as a day alone. Indeed, he emphasizes how these two aspects of life impact each other when he writes, "Let him who cannot be alone fear to be in community; and, let him who cannot be in community, fear to be alone." In order to respond effectively to others, I must maintain a daily discipline of solitude. So too, study is balanced with work, rest, and prayer. These are the rhythms to the balance of a long life of learning.

March 18, 2010

How Do You Bear It???

I frequently hear this question from both students and fellow faculty members alike when I inform them that Sandy and I are living in a studio apartment within the campus Mission House. Their questions reflect the common knowledge that the Mission House studio apartments were originally designed for short-term occupancy by a single individual -- not extended living for a couple. How do you bear living in such close-quarters? I also hear the same question -- So, how do you bear it? -- from friends and family, when they ask about our adjusting to life in a culture that is in so many ways "upside-down" from what a modern American is use to in this day and age. Not that we are experiencing "primitive living" in any way, shape or form -- our son Caleb would quickly attest to the many "modern" conveniences (like electric power and gas heat) that we daily are dependent upon -- but many of the "customary" life practices here leave us feeling very "foreign."

One experience this past week brought this question to mind in a particular manner. I was invited as a member of the undergraduate law faculty to attend the law student association's "MT" -- "membership training" session. I was informed that a bus would be provided to transport everyone from campus to a dining facility off-campus where we would enjoy a meal followed by the MT session. The bus was to depart campus at 6:30pm on Friday and, I was told, would not return until 2am. What did you just say? 2am? I heard correctly, for such are the "bonding" experiences of students here -- which, if I think about it for a few minutes, is not unlike the late night excursions of university students in the States or in whatever country, for that matter -- but, did they really want their professors to hang-out with them? Well, . . . yeah. I was even treated to a seven course meal, prepared by the leaders of the student association, no less.

And then, we were all directed to a fellowship hall on a lower level of the building where a worship service was held. Prof. Chi, the chairman of the School of Law, presented a challenging message from the story of Micaiah, the prophet who spoke truth to power even though all the other 400 prophets affirmed the evil King Ahab's plan. He reminded us that "bearing witness to the truth" in our efforts to "do justice" may often prove costly in our careers and even to our lives.

I was reminded by Prof. Chi's words of what Jesus had said to his disciples: "For truly, I say to you, whoever gives you a cup of water to drink because you bear the name of Christ, will by no means lose his reward." (Mark 9:41, emphasis added). Now the question came to me in a much different way – How do you bear it? That is, how do I bear the name of Christ? Do I bear it well, or do I bear it poorly? That I "bear it" at all is only by the gift of God's abundant grace. But, I would do well to examine myself regularly with this question. If I claim to be a Christ-follower, how am I doing bearing his name? Interestingly, the first followers of The Way (Acts 9:2) did not take on the name "Christian" (literally "little Christ's"). Rather, they were called Christians in the town of Antioch. (Acts 11:26) Others recognized that they were following the life and teachings of Jesus Christ and so called them by his name. Is that how I have come to bear his name?

How am I bearing it, today?

Note: I didn't end-up staying at the MT until 2am. One of my good and faithful colleagues, Prof. Cheoljoon Chang, graciously offered me a ride back to campus around 11pm. I have already found that when one has to bear with sleeplessness, it is an even greater challenge to bear the name. The spirit is indeed willing, but the flesh is weak.

March 31, 2010

Counter in Every Culture

One of Mark Twain's most thought-provoking and critical commentaries on life in his day was the delightful novel "A Connecticut Yankee in King Arthur's Court." In many ways these days, I feel as though I may very well be living the tale of "A Missouri Boarder on President Kim's Campus." (Folks, like me, from Missouri are neither "Yankees" nor "Rebels" since ours was a "border" state). For, even after nearly six months of attempted assimilation, I still find myself often "at odds" with the expectations and practices of my new surrounding culture.

Many of the practices and behaviors that I'm told are "cultural," though, seem to be in actuality characteristic of human nature in every culture. What might appear to be a rude, assertive pushing to the head of the line is really not so much a manifestation of a cultural tendency as it is an evidence of a self-focus that is common to humanity as a whole -- and, that whole clearly includes me. The splinters that I've so meticulously identified in the many dark eyes about me are truly fragments of the burgeoning beam protruding from my own. What I'm coming to understand, however, is that a life seeking to be lived according to the teachings and practices of Christ will, in very many respects, be counter in every culture that it encounters. I believe this is true because so much of what we defend and even attempt to protect as "culture" is all too often an institutionalization of human behaviors that are, by their very nature, at odds with the life we humans were originally designed and created to live with one another.

Behaviors that are frequently accommodated by playing the "culture card" are in reality the very ones that should instead be targeted for transformation. Instead of asserting ourselves to positions of higher recognition, we are called to "associate with the lowly." Rather than striving for authority and control over others, we are commanded by Jesus to "love one another as I have loved you." In the place of retaliation and anger when harmed or offended, we are charged to forgive and "bless those who persecute you." Jesus was the ultimate counter to his culture in both his teaching and example. And so his followers should be in theirs.

> *A dispute also arose among them, as to which of them was to be regarded as the greatest. And he said to them, "The kings of the Gentiles exercise lordship over them, and those in authority over them are called benefactors. But not so with you. Rather, let the greatest among you become as the youngest, and the leader as one who serves. For who is the greater, one who reclines at table or one who serves? Is it not the one who reclines at table? But I am among you as the one who serves.* (Luke 22:24-27)

11

April 6, 2010

A Teacher's Dilemma

One of my students recently posed a question that prompted me to pause and think. The student attends my Tuesday and Friday morning class on Legal Argumentation. The purpose of this course is to sharpen both the students' analytical thinking and their legal writing and speaking skills. I had given the class their first writing assignment -- a research memorandum. I emphasized the importance of their writing in a clear, concise and convincing manner. I also stressed to the class the importance of choosing the right words in arguing the position they had determined was correct. Finally, I charged them to observe the wisdom of the Chinese proverb that you see written at right. It reads: "Fewer words are best." I'd been told that it may also be translated: "Fewer words are beautiful." It was this last bit of writing advice that confused my student and gave rise to her question.

"I thought you were supposed to be teaching us to write like lawyers. Why do you say that we should use fewer words? I thought lawyers always used a lot of words." I had to admit that her understanding of lawyers -- and American lawyers, in particular -- was indeed correct. Lawyers are professionals who use words -- lots of words -- to make their point and advance their clients' interests. In fact, I have often admitted to my students that as a recovering lawyer, I suffer from a professional disability -- I talk too much. In a meager attempt at self-justification, I offer the weak excuse that after ten years of a law practice where I essentially got paid by the word, I developed the nasty habit. But, my student's question presented me with a dilemma. To teach effective writing and speaking skills, I have to use words. But the more words I use, I am actually doing the very thing I'm trying to teach my students to avoid. If I use fewer words, I fear my teaching will be ineffective; if I use more words, though, I won't be able to demonstrate the principal lesson of the course. What's a teacher to do?

Is it possible to teach, write and speak effectively with fewer words? The wisdom of that Chinese proverb is consistent with the teaching of Scripture. James admonishes us to be "quick to hear, slow to speak." (James 1:19) Solomon, too, teaches us: "Be not rash with your mouth, nor let your heart be hasty to utter a word before God, for God is in heaven and you are on earth. Therefore let your words be few. For a dream comes with much business, and a fool's voice with many words." (Ecclesiastes 5:2-3). And finally, Jesus himself warns us that "on the day of judgment people will give account for every careless word they speak." (Matthew 12:36)

If I am to follow these instructions, I will need to slow down and choose my words with care. Yes, it is possible to be an effective communicator with fewer words, but it takes time. In fact, it takes more time to compose an argument in a clear, concise and convincing manner than it does to come up with one twice as long. Thus, I must be slow, not hasty, to speak a few careful, not careless, words. I don't know if my student realized how telling her question was. It prompted me to remember to practice first before I seek to teach.

April 14, 2010

My Testimony to God's Grace, Mercy and Faithfulness

Last week, the campus pastor asked me to give my testimony at the weekly faculty chapel service that was held this morning. I thought it best to write out my story in order to keep the telling of it under the twenty-five minutes I had been allotted. Here is what I said:

My parents were devout Lutherans. So, shortly after my birth, they had me baptized in their home congregation, Immanuel Lutheran Church in Boonville, Missouri. I was confirmed in the Lutheran faith at age 13 and expressed an interest in studying for the ministry at that time. Although I had an "academic" understanding of the person of Christ through my upbringing in the church and even an inclination to pursue the ministry, it was not until my freshman year of high school that I came to personal faith in the Lord Jesus. My algebra teacher spoke with me one day after class and asked me if I was saved. He also pointed me to a number of Bible passages that spoke about a personal relationship with God through the Lord Jesus Christ. He encouraged me not only to read God's Word, but also to study it seriously. I began to attend Bible studies at my teacher's home on a weekly basis and also during my lunch break from school in the basement of a Baptist church across the street from the high school. I developed friendships with believers from a variety of evangelical and reformed churches. After about one year of study, I came to place my trust in Christ's work alone for my salvation.

At this point in my life I began to study the Scriptures with an even greater intensity and seriousness. I attended St. Paul's College High, a Lutheran school located in Concordia, Missouri, for my remaining two years of high school. My direction, though, changed from ministerial training to Christian education, and I made a decision to resign my membership in the Lutheran church in order to fellowship with a small group of believers who met as an assembly of Plymouth Brethren. My decision to leave the Lutheran church was extremely hard on my father whose family had been Lutheran for generations. I did not, however, realize the extent of his disappointment at the time. Instead, I was being significantly influenced by my reading of the biographies of both George Mueller and Jim Elliot. In addition, while attending a church youth retreat in St. Louis at the South Side Bible Chapel, I met the young lady, Sandy White, who would later become my wife. Throughout this formative period in my life, my parents continued to support me and gave their blessing for both my upcoming marriage to Sandy and our decision to go into full-time ministry as a school teacher with Victory Christian School operated by South Side Bible Chapel, the Plymouth Brethren assembly where Sandy had grown-up and where we would be members.

In August of 1978, Sandy and I were married at South Side and in that same month, the church ordained me to full-time ministry as a teacher at Victory even though I had not yet completed my undergraduate education. I continued to take classes at local colleges during my two years of teaching middle school students at Victory. During these years of teaching, I developed a particular interest in the many legal issues facing Christian schools and ministries, as well as parents who were seeking to home school their children. After consulting with a number of older brothers and my parents, my wife and I decided to move to South Carolina where I enrolled in Bob Jones University in order to pursue a pre-law course of studies. I believed that the Lord was now leading me to serve others through becoming a lawyer. So, Sandy and I and our 7-month old son, Caleb, traveled over 700 miles to a new place away from our families for the first time.

We spent three years in South Carolina. In addition to my studies at university and working a full-time job, we were actively involved in our local church another Plymouth Brethren assembly -- where I served in both the preaching and teaching of the Word.

Upon graduation, and the growth of our family to three children, we returned to St. Louis in the summer of 1983. We renewed our fellowship with the believers at South Side, and I entered law school at Saint Louis University. During my three years in law school, I continued to serve my church through preaching and teaching. My ministries also expanded to working with college-aged young people. At law school, I assisted with the establishment of a local chapter of the Christian Legal Society and led Bible studies on campus.

After graduating from law school in May 1986 and passing the bar later that summer, I joined a large firm in downtown St. Louis to provide for my wife and now family of four children – our youngest, Justin Mark, had been born in the middle of my second year at law school. I had started the professional stage of my life journey. Still believing that God has called me to use my profession to serve others, I attempted to develop a practice in the area of First Amendment law. I found, however, that the demands and restrictions of being an associate in one of the largest law firms in St. Louis did not complement my pursuits. Instead, I became distracted by the wiles of "big firm" practice, and after about six years, I was nearly consumed by the world. All the while, though, I continued outwardly to serve in my local church. I was drawing near to God with my lips, but my heart was growing farther and farther away from him. Through a series of challenging circumstances over the next three years of my law practice, I began to experience deeper and deeper bouts of depression largely due to my leading a duplicitous life.

At one point, I remember distinctly driving my car into the parking garage of the office building where I was working, and as I drove down into the garage, I felt as if darkness itself was completely enveloping me. It was my Psalm 88:18 experience. Do you know that verse? I think it must be one of the saddest verses in the Bible. Heman the Erzahite sighs and says to God: "You have caused my beloved and my friend to shun me; my companions have become darkness." I turned my car around, drove straight back to the big two-story colonial house I had had built to show all my friends how successful a lawyer I had become, got out of my car, went into the house and went back to bed. Sandy was concerned that I was ill, but I told that I didn't know what was wrong with me. I didn't want to do anything; I didn't want to talk to anyone; I just wanted to go back to bed. She left me there for several hours, but later she came back to the bedroom and said to me: "I don't know what is wrong with you. I only know that you need to get back to doing what you used to do." By that, she meant, I needed to get back to reading God's Word on a daily basis and journaling my thoughts and ideas, my prayers and concerns. A few days later, by the grace of God, I started back to doing what I had been taught to do in the early years of my walk with Lord.

I was restored in my faith through meditation upon Scripture, prayer and the discipline of journaling. Within the next few months, I ended up leaving that large law firm I had been working for the past nine years, and joining a small firm of Christian lawyers. In January, 1995, my family and I also decided to move our church fellowship to a small gathering of believers who met at place providentially called Grace Bible Chapel. This transfer out of "law" and into "grace" was accompanied by my desire and interest to return to full-time ministry. The elders at Grace Bible Chapel invited me to spend a year praying with them about an opportunity for me to serve in a pastoral-teaching ministry within the church. That year turned into 18 months, after which the church ordained me in May 1996.

Having now left behind the practice of law, yet another stage in my journey had begun. Over the next four years, I committed myself to ministry in the local church. My elders also encouraged me to start theological studies at Covenant Seminary, and I continued there as a part-time student for the next seven years. During that same time period, I also started teaching on a part-time basis at Missouri Baptist University as a lecturer in law. In January, 2000, the

University offered me a full-time appointment to its faculty as an assistant professor. This marked a new stage in my journey. The course of my life over 25 years to that point had been marked by my respective callings to teaching, law and ministry. These three strands were brought together in the opportunity to serve on the faculty of Missouri Baptist. I began teaching as an assistant professor of Interdisciplinary Studies. Later, I was appointed Chair of the Division of Social & Behavioral Sciences and then, Associate Academic Dean of Undergraduate Studies.

The high-light of my years of teaching at Missouri Baptist was the opportunity I was given to develop a senior seminar focusing students on critical thinking and analytical writing skills. The course required the students to read broadly and to consider what it meant to live an examined, an integrated and an offered life according to one's calling. The theme of this course became the challenge I would use to conclude every class session of every course I have taught from then until now: Question Everything! Hold on to the Good! In the fall of 2003, I had the privilege of meeting two professors from Handong while presenting a paper at an academic conference in Florida. Those two were Professor Hee Eun Lee and Professor Guk Woon "Kuyper" Lee. They told me about a young university in Korea called Handong, and they invited me to apply for a summer visiting professorship.

The next summer, after completing my seminary studies at Covenant, I traveled here to Korea for the first time and taught a course on Antitrust Law at Handong International Law School. Upon my return to St. Louis that fall, I continued to serve on the faculty at Missouri Baptist until August, 2005 when I began teaching as a part-time lecturer at Fontbonne University and also started my PhD studies in Theology & Culture at Concordia Seminary. For the next two years while teaching and studying, I also served as a chaplain to the legal community in St. Louis, Missouri through the Christian Legal Society's Spirit of St. Louis Pilot Project in Marketplace Discipleship. In conjunction with this ministry, I was ordained as a pastor of discipleship by my current home church, West Hills Community Church. After completing that project, I continued to teach part-time as a Senior Lecturer at Fontbonne University as well as study in the Theology & Culture PhD program at Concordia Seminary. Last summer, I received an invitation to come back here to Handong as a visiting professor of American Law in the undergraduate School of Law's U.S. and International Law program.

God has led me on a long journey. It has taken many turns -- from my Lutheran family upbringing, through the Plymouth Brethren to now serving at a Baptist church. Along the way I have been a student at a Fundamentalist University – Bob Jones, a Jesuit Law School – Saint Louis University, both a Presbyterian and Lutheran Seminary – Covenant and Concordia. I've taught at a Southern Baptist and a Catholic University – Missouri Baptist and Fontbonne – and now, for this academic year – I teaching here at Handong.

All in all, as I look back over my nearly 51 years upon this earth, I realize anew that it has only been the grace, mercy and faithfulness of God through Christ Jesus that has brought me through. I continue to look forward to the opportunities for service that the Lord has yet ahead of me as I continue to seek, by His grace and strength, to fulfill both His calling to teach and His purpose through serving others in this my generation. I can confidently say, as I know you too will confess, that it is only: "By the grace of God [that] I am what I am, and his grace toward me was not in vain."

> *If the LORD had not been my help,*
> *my soul would soon have lived in the land of silence.*
> *When I thought, "My foot slips,"*
> *your steadfast love, O LORD, held me up.*
> *When the cares of my heart are many,*
> *your consolations cheer my soul.*
>
> (Psalm 94: 17-19)

April 29, 2010

Bodily Exercise Profits (a) Little

One of the benefits of living on a campus with nearly 4000 young people is the constant motivation you sense to be active and even a feeling of guilt for being so out-of-shape. This impression comes home to you when you get up at 6:30am each morning to set out on your daily "walk-about" the campus only to find that teams of students have already been up for almost an hour (since the sunrise) and are vigorously engaged in battle upon the soccer pitch that occupies the better part of the center of campus. If only I had the energy and stamina to be out there running around and kicking that ball!

Well, Sandy must have picked-up on those unspoken expressions by means of her feminine intuition. How do I know? She hired one of the seniors on campus to be our personal trainer! His name is Aleksey. He's a national judo champion from Uzbekistan. Not only is he in spectacular physical shape, he also speaks four languages -- Uzbek, Russian, Korean and English -- so his mind is as fit as his body! Now, every Wednesday and Friday evenings, we meet Aleksey in the campus health club -- located on the basement level of Shalom Dormitory -- for our training sessions. They begin with warm-ups and a series of stretches. We then proceed to running on the treadmill for about 12-15 minutes at various levels of speed. Aleksey is working us up to 8 km/h, but at this point -- three weeks into our training -- we're doing well to make it to 6 km/h -- a nice jogging pace. Then comes the squats. Three sets of 10 rep's each by the end of which the tops of my thighs are beginning to burn with pain. But, we're only about half-way through our program.

Next, Aleksey demonstrates three floor exercises. The first one requires us to lie on our backs, pull our heads up at 30 degrees, fix our eyes on a point on the wall, and then lift our legs up and then lower them down -- slowly -- until they are about two inches off the floor, and then lift them back up again. We repeat this exercise 6 to 8 rep's for two sets. Now, lie back and bring your heels toward your bottom so that your knees are raised up about 12-14 inches; extend your arms placing your hands on the tops of your thighs and then raise up siding your hands up toward your knee caps and hold it there! Gently, lie back and repeat this exercise now 6 to 8 times for two sets. Tired yet? I forgot to tell you that in between each set of exercises you are to get up and walk around in order to keep yourself loose all the while controlling your breathing with long and deep inhalations followed by slow exhalations. Now, back down on the floor -- this time on your stomach. Bring your knees up under you with your palms flat on the floor in front. Gradually extend your legs back while you arch your stomach in and your head back almost forming a C with your body. Got the picture? Now do that 6 to 8 times for two sets.

We're nearly through. At this point, we move to the exercise machines. The first one requires us to sit in a chair and place our feet on a platform that is connected to a set of pulleys. The cable running through the pulleys is connected to a series of weights that allows you to increase and decrease the amount of weight that your legs will be lifting as you push the platform with your feet. We start with 20 kilos and gradually move up to 30 and then 40. Finally, we head over to the last apparatus. This one is a bit tough to describe – not because it is particularly complex, but because it requires your body to bend and stretch in ways that are not a part of the normal range of physical activities you might encounter in an ordinary day.

Here's the scene – first you place your thighs on pads that are set at about a 45 degree angle. Then, you place your heels up against a set of rollers. This essentially locks the lower half of your body into a slanted position. Now arch your back up with your hands raised up in the surrender posture (because at this point in the training you are ready to say, "I give up!" – but you don't). Instead, you slowly lower the upper half of your body down farther and farther until you are now making an A frame with the highest point of the A being your bottom – you feet form on base and your head is the other base of the A. Now, raise-up slowly (inhaling along the way) back up to the arching position. Repeat this movement 6 to 8 times for two sets. Did you survive? Aleksey keeps a close watch on us so we don't overdo it. One time last week, though, Sandy couldn't make it to the training session, so I was working on my own with Aleksey. Another one of my international faculty colleagues, Alex from Australia, was also doing a workout in the gym on some nearby equipment. He happened to overhear me say to Aleksey that I wasn't feeling as sore as I thought I might be this the level of training I had been through thus far. Alex, looking out for my best interests, shouted over, "Don't say that Mate! Yaur trainer will pushya even haawrrder!"

Needless to say, that was the last time I made any comments about not feeling sore. In fact, it was the last time I've not been feeling sore as I'm finding that this bodily exercise is profiting – a little, so far, though, a very little.

12

May 1, 2010

A Letter of Decision

For the past five months, I have been seeking God's guidance concerning my future. What follows is a letter that I wrote and presented earlier this week to the chairman of Handong's School of Law faculty.

Dear Professor Chi,

At the end of the 2009 fall semester, you extended to me the University's invitation to apply for a full-time professorship. At that time, I stated that I believed it would be wise for me to wait until near the end of the spring semester to make a decision in response to the University's invitation. I wanted to have additional time to learn more about Handong and to seek God's guidance concerning my future academic service. I also wanted to give my wife the opportunity to come here to Handong so that she might experience life with me on the campus and meet both my fellow faculty members and students.

Throughout this semester, my wife and I have been praying for God's direction and wisdom regarding our future. We have had many long talks about my service at Handong. We have also talked about the needs of our children and grand children back in the United States. During my visit to the United States during the Christmas holiday break, I also had the opportunity to meet with members of the administration of Fontbonne University where I have been teaching for the past five years prior to my visiting professorship at Handong this year. Lastly, I met with my Doktorvater at Concordia Seminary where I am currently working on PhD studies.

Based upon these extended times of prayer and conversation, as well as my meetings with both Fontbonne University and Concordia Seminary in January, I have decided to accept an offer from Fontbonne University to return to my teaching post in St. Louis, Missouri, this coming fall term. I will also be returning to complete my PhD studies at Concordia Seminary. I believe that this is the best course for me to follow in serving God's purpose according to His call upon my life as a teacher, husband, father and grandfather at this time in my life. As a result of this decision, I will be concluding my service as a visiting professor at Handong at the end of the current spring semester.

My teaching experiences here at Handong these past two semesters have been wonderful. I am very thankful that the Lord has given me the privilege of serving together with you and my other esteemed colleagues on the faculty of the School of Law. I am very interested in maintaining an on-going working relationship with Handong Global University. I would look forward to opportunities to return in the future for additional terms of teaching should the occasion arise for the University to request my service again in a visiting professorship capacity.

Please accept my most grateful thanks for your leadership and for the opportunity to serve the students of Handong Global University as we together seek the will of God and His Kingdom.

May 6, 2010

Set Your Seal

There are many things that fascinate me about Asian culture. I believe my interest in Asia, in general, and in the countries of China and Korea, in particular, dates back to my elementary school days when my father was member of the local Rotary Club in Boonville, Missouri. One of the regular events that dad's Rotary Club sponsored was a series of films shown at the high school auditorium called the Travelog. Each month a different film would be shown about places around the world that folks from Boonville had never heard of and would be even more likely to never be able to visit. I recall several films over the years that featured China, Korea and other exotic countries of the East. One film documented life in the small Himalayan country of Hunza. It is located near Tibet and is one of those countries that many travelers believe may have inspired stories about Shangri La.

I imagine that those stories and films of Asia were the earliest seeds that grew my increasing interest in this land over the years. In particular, I have always been intrigued by Asian calligraphy. I remember once when I was a teenager purchasing a wall scroll at an Asian imports store in Columbia, Missouri, located next door to the health foods grocery where my parents would frequently shop. I don't think I realized at the time that the scroll I had purchased was written in Korean Hangul. The Hangul alphabet, as well as the intricacies of Chinese characters, continues to fascinate me. On our recent trip to Seoul, I discovered several hand-made paper and stamp shops in the Insadon traditional shopping district. One of the customs of Asian writing is to sign one's name with a special seal that is always inked with a particular hue of red. I asked my faithful teaching assistant, Mr. Mok, to order a signature stamp with my name in Korean Hangul. That's the stamp in the upper right corner of this post. It reads: 코(Ko)델(Del)슐(Schul)튼(Teun).

Now, I can "set my seal" in Korean upon any document I write. This is one of the many Korean customs that I will bring back with me to the States. These months that I lived here have definitely had a formative impact upon me, and I trust that the forming that has and is taking place is for the better -- as my thinking is broadened and my experience of life deepened.

May 9, 2010

A Red-Letter Day

The 5th of May is a national holiday in Korea. On every Korean calendar the date is highlighted in red. Its Children's Day. Everyone gets the day off from work to spend the entire day with their children. Here on campus all classes were cancelled, and even the weekly faculty meetings that are ordinarily held every Wednesday were postponed until next week. Most of the faculty members plan outings with their families at the local park or hikes into the foothills of the surrounding mountains.

A few of my Law & Advocacy Study Group students had learned that May 5 was also my birthday, so they invited Sandy and me to a brunch at Hyoam Restaurant. I wasn't exactly sure what would be on the bunch menu, but I was looking forward to an enjoyable, leisurely morning with some of my brightest students. When we arrived at the Restaurant, though, I was a bit confused to find that none of my students had shown-up. Koreans generally tend to be somewhat late to events, but when students plan a meal for their professor they usually arrive well in advance to make preparations.

The owner of the restaurant must have noticed that I was puzzled, so he suggested that Sandy and I should wait in the special dining room and assured me that my students were "on their way." About ten minutes later -- as we were considering putting out a call to the study group leader -- the doors on both ends of the dining room opened, and my students processed in singing the traditional Korean birthday song to a guitar accompaniment. The song was followed by the presentation of a beautifully decorated cake sporting one, tall and thin, lit candle. As I accepted the cake, the whole group together sang "Happy Birthday to You" in English. At the end of the song, they all encouraged me to blow-out the single candle. They explained that, while they knew this was not my first birthday (by a long shot, a 50-year long shot), it was the first of my birthday's to be celebrated in Korea. They wished for me to celebrate many more birthdays here at Handong in the future. Some already knew of our decision to return to the States this summer, but they were still attempting to use their influence to persuade me to stay longer.

Next, I was presented with a rice paper scroll from Prof. Chi, the chairman of the School of Law, on which he had hand-painted in Chinese calligraphy the characters Ko Deok which one student translated for me as "high character" or "practicing the highest good". It is the name that Prof. Chi has given to me. Another of my students then presented me with a gift box (about 8 inches x 8 inches x 5 inches in size) in which I found some 50 small pieces of orange paper all rolled-up in scrolls. I later unrolled each of the orange scrolls to find a special individual birthday wish written by my students. Some expressed their wishes in their language and provided me with a translation, others even drew pictures.

The final gift was presented when we all took our seats around the tables. I had cut the cake for everyone to enjoy, but just before I could take a bite, Ms. Han -- the leader of my student study group -- placed in front of me a bowl of traditional Korean birthday soup that she had prepared herself. It consists of a broth with a healthy amount of seaweed, an excellent source of nutrients, topped with a small portion of beef. Along with the soup, a bowl of rice is also served. The soup is an expression of everyone's wish that the one celebrating his birthday experience a long and healthy life. I ate nearly all of it before moving on to the less-than-health-enhancing (but delicious) cake. Needless to say, I was quite overwhelmed by the thoughtfulness and kindness of my students and fellow colleagues. It will be a birthday celebration that I will long remember -- a true red-letter day!

May 16, 2010

Look Out for Them Thar Boars!

That's what I said, "Boars!" -- as in wild pigs! I couldn't believe my eyes when I looked out the back window of our apartment late Saturday afternoon. At first, I could only make out some movement in the tall grass that had overgrown the rice fields in the valley immediately behind the Mission House. I was drawn, though, to watch. There was something out there. In a matter of minutes, he came into the clearing, or at least, I'm pretty sure it was a he. It was a boar! He was as big as any pig I had ever seen back in Missouri. But he had something those hogs did not. He had a mane of short, stiff, black hair running from the top of his head to the middle of his back -- the sign of what an Arkansan would call a "razorback."

But then, I realized that this big guy was not alone. There was a second dark and equally big boar rooting around, too . . . and three more young pigs. A whole family of wild boar had come out of the woods to root for their evening dinner in our "backyard." We haven't experienced much of Korean native wildlife, so this was quite a sight. I tried to take a picture -- just in case some of my more skeptical readers might be supposing that I've gone to composing fiction just to liven up our last few weeks here. When I recounted this little adventure to my mother in a telephone conversation this morning, she highly recommended that we not take any more hikes up into the hills behind the Mission House, unless of course, we were well-armed with a big stick. Look-out for them thar boars!

May 19, 2010

Some Thoughts from a Visitor

Shortly after I arrived at Handong last August, I was asked by the student newspaper to write a brief essay describing my initial impressions as a visiting professor. Occasionally, a view from the outside can be a help to enlighten those on the inside. In that first article, I focused on some early experiences with my U.S. & International Law (UIL) students whom I found needed to be encouraged to pose questions in class. I suggested that asking questions is not a sign of disrespect or inattention, but rather, a good question is actually the most authentic signal that a student is truly interested in understanding the deeper meaning of things and not just memorizing facts that will quickly lose their significance once the class exam has passed.

Now, as I come even more quickly to the conclusion of my visiting professorship, I've been asked to reflect back and recount some lessons I've learned during my sojourn here – lessons that I will take back with me when I return to teaching at Fontbonne University this fall in St. Louis. While those lessons have occurred on nearly a daily basis, I believe they may be best expressed in a few words. Through my days of service among you as a teacher, I have learned anew, from experiences with students and colleagues alike, the value of a walking-paced life, the value of interruptions, and the value of listening.

Coming from the States, one of my greatest challenges here arose from my nearly in-born tendency to live life at a rapid pace. Multi-tasking is considered a mark of proficiency. During my time at Handong, though, I have been put in a position where I lived within a short 5-minute walk to where I worked and worshipped. Leading a walking-paced life slows you down. It prompts you to be more reflective about what you do and even what you say.

You also can discover more opportunities to think when you slow down. The life I had been living in the States could fairly be described as a "driving-paced life" that frequently filled me with tension, stress, and worries. At a walking-pace, life may more readily become an on-going occasion for prayer trusting that Christ will lead us step-by-step as we seek to follow him all the days of our life.

Another challenge facing me came from a personality trait that is often inbred in people with my ethnic heritage (i.e. German as the "Sch" in my surname signals). That personality trait is one that insists upon orderliness and precision, especially in my daily schedule. I usually approach each day with a pre-determined plan for nearly every hour. What I often found, though, was that my "plan" was interrupted by knocks on my door or emails announcing meetings for me to attend, not next week, but within a few hours. To say that these interruptions caused me a bit of consternation would be to put it mildly. But, when I allowed the "interruptions" to change my plans, I found that instead of keeping me from doing what I thought I needed to do, pausing to heed those "interruptions" was actually what I was supposed to do. Being ready and willing to respond to the requests of others resulted in greater meaning for that day.

Likely the biggest challenge, though, that confronted me arose from neither the pace of my life nor the pattern of my day. Instead, it stemmed from my ever-present propensity to talk, and to talk too much. In my professional career, I have been a lawyer, a pastor and a professor. Each of these vocations is a "talking" profession. From my months here at Handong, I learned that well-spoken words have an essential prerequisite – thoughtful, engaged listening. I learned once again the value of being quick to hear and slow to speak. I also learned anew (and tried to convey to my students) that when I do speak fewer words are best. These are the lessons that I will take with me from my time of teaching and learning here

– slow down, pause and listen. What I hope to leave to my students and colleagues at Handong is this seven-word admonition: Question everything! Hold on to the good!

May 29, 2010

Two Weddings and a Talent Show

Earlier this month, Sandy and I were invited to attend the weddings of two teachers from the KEBS Sunday School class that we help to teach at The Joyful Church in Pohang. Pictured above is our friend Samuel and his new bride. Their parents stand together on each side of them as they are presented to their 500+ guests as husband and wife for the first time. Korean weddings are very elaborate affairs. Both of the weddings we attended (one on Saturday and the other on Sunday afternoon) were held in the Grand Ballroom of the Philos Hotel -- the biggest hotel in Pohang.

In between these two formal events, we were invited to serve as judges that Saturday night for the University's International Student Union "Open-Mic" talent show. Our trainer, Aleksey, was among the many contestants. As a graduating senior this semester, he sang a parting song that brought tears to many of the young ladies' eyes. I was happy when the other five judges agreed with me that Aleksey was clearly one of the top performers of the night. He won second place! I was called upon to announce the winners and hand-out their prizes.

We enjoyed a full weekend of celebration and quite a bit of fun! There was a striking similarity, though, between the weddings and the talent show. All three were very much staged "productions." At both weddings, special songs were sung by friends of the bride and groom. The second wedding even featured a singer who is well-known in Korean popular culture. The weddings themselves were performed in the midst of banquet tables at which many of the guests had already begun to eat and drink even as the ceremony was occurring. The weddings were, however, distinctly marked by the honor given to the parents of the bride and groom in Korean culture. At the point in the wedding ceremony when American bride's and groom's would give roses to their mothers, the newly wed Korean couple is instructed by the presiding minister to turn first to the parents of the groom and bow. The bride bows from the waist so that her upper body is at nearly a 90 degree angle to her lower body. The groom, however, goes down on his knees and then bows with his arms extended out in front of him along the floor and with his face all the way down to the ground.

After bowing to the parents of the groom, the couple comes across to the parents of the bride and the same bowing ritual is performed in their honor. The value and respect such actions showed to the parents of the married couple was definitely the hallmark of the ceremonies and what -- in the midst of a fun and entertaining weekend -- we will remember most from these two weddings and a talent show.

13

June 6, 2010

Hahoe Village -- The Williamsburg of Korea

One of our last opportunities to experience the wonder and beauty of Korean culture this semester was provided to Sandy and me when my Teaching Assistant, Mr. Mok, and his girl friend Narang, treated us to a day of touring in Andong -- one of the most traditional cities in Korea. The high-light of the trip was the our visit to Hahoe Folk Village. Hahoe is one of the most well-preserved traditional villages in the entire country. The descendants of one family -- the Ryu's -- have lived in this village for over 600 years. Although they have added some modern updates -- electricity and plumbing, as well as automobiles and tractors -- the homes and other structures within the village are authentic. As we walked toward the village on a path through the surrounding wooded hills, I realized that we were about to enter the "Colonial Williamsburg" of Korea.

Just inside the primary entrance to the village, we came upon this example of a traditional home. This is actually just the front gate entrance to the family's compound. It consists of restored and updated structures owned by the CEO of a large Korean corporation. Our guide told that the reconstruction costs were in excess of $5 million US. Each of the established (wealthy) family homes is actually a compound of several buildings enclosed by a stone wall. Within the walls there will be a main dwelling for the women of the family, another dwelling for the men, dwelling for the servants usually built onto the interior side of the surrounding wall. Most of the family compounds will also have a Guest House. Within the walls of the next family compound, this calligrapher had set up a tent and would gladly write a word of phase of your choosing. I asked him to write the name that my department chair, Profressor Chi, had given me: 高德

Situated at the very center of Hahoe Village is this 600-year old zelkova tree which the villagers call "Samsindang". The name means "shrine for three gods." According to traditional animistic beliefs, the tree is worshipped as a spirit. On the 15th of every January (by the lunar calendar), the villagers perform a ritual at the tree to pray for the peace of the village. When I was walking back along one of the paths, this little sparrow caught my attention. It reminded me that no matter where you go in the world, you always find sparrows. And when I remember what Jesus taught. Not one sparrow falls to ground without the Father's knowledge. And as God cares for the sparrows, you can be assured He cares for you. You are worth more than many sparrows.

Yangjindang, one of the oldest houses in Hahoe Village, belongs to the head of the Ryu clan in the P'ungsan area. It is one of the Korean national treasures. Ryu, Seong-ryong (1542-1607), a famous court minister who helped protect Korea from the Japanese invasion of 1592, lived here. I made the grievous mistake, though, of stepping-up on the wooden deck structure that surrounds the outside of the building. The sign warning against stepping-up was written in Korean only. I should, however, have asked our guide before stepping-up and taking these pictures. My offense resulted in one of the other Korean visitors (who had observed my disrespectful conduct) giving me a sound chewing-out as I was later told by our guide.

Just a few kilometers down the Nakdong River is located Dosan Confucian Academy, one of the oldest in Korea. At the top of these stairs is the entry gate to the shrine within the academy's grounds that was built to house the memorial tablet of Yi Hwang (이황). Yi is one of Korea's most celebrated philosophers. At the end of this very full and inspiring day, our guide, Young Ju Choi, bid us a warm farewell. We thoroughly enjoyed our visit to the "Williamsburg" of Korea.

June 11, 2010

Let Us Not Love in Words or Talk, but . . . .

"Let us love with deeds and in truth," so said the Apostle John when writing in the first century to followers of Jesus. (1 John 3:18) His words speak to the heart of a problem that has recently come into sharper focus for me here. That problem is the human intendancy to "talk a lot" about how we love others but actually to do very little true acts of love. I realize that this is a problem in my own life, and it appears to be a present deficiency in large number of professing followers of Christ today.

The idea that we can love merely in words is indeed a persistent problem. It came into clearer view for me a few weeks ago when a visitor to our global campus here in Korea made a presentation to students and faculty on the international crimes of human trafficking. Our visitor's stated purpose for her presentation was "to raise awareness" about this tragic reality in our world. She presented an extremely informative lecture with heart-rending photographs of victims of sexual slavery and forced labor. It was a very moving presentation.

During the Q & A session, one very perceptive student asked our visitor what she had done to help free a victim of trafficking. The presenter's reply was quite telling. She acknowledged that there were organizations on the front lines that are engaged in direct efforts to free victims and prosecute the perpetrators of these human rights violations, but that was not something she did.

Instead, she believed her role was to raise awareness about the problem because "she was gifted at talking and making presentations." She also recounted a story about a group of high school students to whom she had given a similar presentation. Following the presentation, the students raised a significant amount of money to send to one of the organizations that is working against human trafficking. There is no doubt that "raising awareness" as well as "raising funding" are important dimensions in the success of any endeavor to address pressing human needs in the world. But the Handong student who first raised the question of what a person can "do" was not satisfied with the presenter's response. She knew that there must be something more.

Is there a willingness on my part to consider whether "awareness" of a need should lead us to ask the more important question: "What can I do?" And am I willing to consider whether the answer to the question of "doing" is not resolved by merely giving money or joining in the effort to "raise awareness" even further? Are we willing to allow for the possibility . . . opening ourselves to a readiness . . . to actually take action by going and being with those whom we are so ready to talk about? Will we consider and seek God's grace to obey the command to "bear the burdens" of others?

Will we begin to move beyond merely "loving" with our words and by talking about the needs of others? Will we begin to love others with deeds that cost us more than a few dollars contributed to a cause? Will we begin to love in truth by going to, being with and bearing the burdens of others?

June 26, 2010

Last Days

I find myself now living in the last days of my sojourn here at Handong. When you know the date of your departure, the last days seem to lengthen. I finished the reading and marking of my last set of student exam papers and have now submitted my student's grades for the semester. I'm nearly packed, but I still find myself wondering whether I'll forget something or whether I'm trying to take too much back to the States. I have distributed out to others nearly two-thirds of the books I had shipped over last August. I invited my students and colleagues to stop by my office over the past two weeks and select two or three books that they had an interest in reading. Some students asked me to write a personal inscription in the book they chose. Others (colleagues on whom I had placed no limit) just took arm-loads. The few that remained were donated to Handong's library.

During these last days, I have also enjoyed the fellowship of both students and colleagues alike who have invited me out to a dinner. One group of students (several from my Law & Advocacy study group/debate team) treated me to a meal at Hyoam Restaurant last week. In the course of our dinner conversation, one student asked if he might be permitted to pose a personal question. Without hesitation, I encouraged him to fire away. He asked me a question that is often put to students at Handong by their professors. The answer that is expected, here at Handong, usually involves the description of a long-term plan for addressing some pressing global need that the student believes he has been called to fulfill as his contribution to changing the world.

His question: What is your vision? The answer I gave, though, did not fit the expected mold. I did not have a grand vision of establishing 300 universities around the developing world (this, however, is an example of the scale of vision that students have come to expect from their professors). Instead, I expressed my desire to be willing to do God's will whatever that might be in the coming days I am given upon this earth. I admitted that I really did not know, with any degree of confidence, what was lying ahead of me. I believed that for now, at least, I am to return to my home in the States and continue to fulfill the callings that God has upon my life as a teacher, husband, son, father, grandfather, and student. I trust that God will lead and provide me with the grace and strength to do what he wills for each day.

I expressed my aspiration in the words that the Apostle Paul used to describe the life of King David. I said that I will have fulfilled my vision if it can be said by others of me at the end of my life that I "served the purpose of God in my own generation." (Acts 13:36). As I now come closer to the last of my days here in Korea (for the time being, at least), I am realizing in a deeper way, I trust, the importance of keeping a willingness to do his will as my singular vision.

August 3, 2010

Concluding Thoughts

I've now been back in the States for five weeks. Much of my time since returning has been spent with my mother who still lives in my hometown in central Missouri. She has been experiencing some health issues which at 81 years of age can be quite debilitating. I've been thankful that I have been able to be near, help and encourage her. My days with her have affirmed God's direction for me at this time.

During my visits with my mother, I've also have been afforded a considerable amount of quite time. So among other studies, I've been reading Eric Metaxas' new biography on Bonhoffer. It gives some wonderful insights into the daily life and struggles

Bonhoeffer encountered, especially in the mid to late 1930's, as he sought to learn and do what he believed to be God's will for his life. Bonhoeffer's view of the Scripture comes through quite vividly as he writes to his family and friends regarding his decisions. Bonhoeffer believed that God desired to and did speak very personally to his servants through his Word. He read the Scriptures daily with an anticipation of God's revelation to him -- not, however, of some new or extra-biblical idea, but of God's will for him. When pondering whether to stay in America in the summer of 1939 as Germany under Hitler was on the verge of war, Bonhoeffer read Isaiah 28:16, "The one who believes does no flee" and became convinced that to remain in America was "to flee" from his responsibility before God in Germany.

He decided to leave the safety and security of America and return as soon as possible to his homeland. A few days later he read 2 Timothy 4 - "Do thy diligence to come before winter" and reflected in his personal journal upon this verse in these words: "Come before winter" -- it is not a misuse of Scripture if I take that to be said to me. If God gives me grace to do it." (Emphasis in the original) (p. 340 in Metaxas). As I think about the way Bonhoeffer lived his life, I am becoming more and more convinced these days that to live a life truly submitted to God's Word, I too must look daily to God in faith with an expectation for his guidance and direction through the revelation of his Word. This will not come by the effort of analyzing the Word with human reason, but through the work of the Holy Spirit in a heart and mind that desires to do God's will.

I believe this is one of the most important lessons that I have been learning during the past year, most of which I have lived abroad at Handong. I am open to return and serve others there in the future as God directs. For now, though, I'll remain here seeking to study, practice and teach God's Word and way by serving others, my mother and family chief among them.

December 15, 2010

Practicing Mindfulness

A few weeks ago I learned that a teaching opportunity that I had been told would be opening for me in St. Louis within the next academic year will, in fact, not be opening. The door to that opportunity seems to be closing or is actually completely closed now. I had been planning on that position, but now it appears that I have a much greater need to practice daily mindfulness rather than living so much for an imagined future whose fulfillment was and is completely out of my hands. In the midst of this time of searching for guidance and reflection upon my calling to teach, I have started to read Thich Nhat Hanh's little book, The Miracle of Mindfulness. Thich Nhat Hanh had a substantial impact upon Martin Luther King, Jr. Dr. King even nominated him for the Nobel Peace Prize for his leadership in the movement for peace in Vietnam during the 1960's.

I was first introduced to the writings of Thich Nhat Hanh by my good friend and colleague, John Han, when I served with him on the faculty of Missouri Baptist University. As I have read, I have been challenged by Hanh's insights in to living a whole life. In this little book, he writes: "Mindfulness is the miracle by which we master and restore ourselves. . . it is the miracle which can call back in a flash our dispersed mind and restore it to wholeness so that we can live each minute of life" (21). Thich Nhat Hanh's instruction on the practice of mindfulness echoes the theme of "single-mindedness" that pervades the New Testament. More than merely a self-discipline, single-mindedness is very much a gift of the Holy Spirit as he is at work forming within each follower of Jesus the mind of Christ. Paul exhorts the disciple of Christ to do whatever your hand finds to do heartily as unto to the Lord (Colossians 3:23) and to do all things to the glory of God. This is practicing mindfulness.

May I be living more wholly in the fullness of my present calling today that I may know and practice such mindfulness in each moment that is granted to me.

December 22, 2010

"Watch and Pray"

I find myself in a time of waiting. As I ponder the options that are before me, I continue to wait on the responses of others to clarify what opportunities are presently open to me. While prayer is always essential to the one who seeks to follow Christ, I'm realizing even more how necessary it is during these times of waiting.

Bonhoeffer's comments on the petition "Thy will be done, as in heaven so on earth" are particularly poignant as I seek to practice living a submitted, singular and sacrificed life. He writes: "In fellowship with Jesus his followers have surrendered their own wills completely to God's, and so they pray that God's will may be done throughout the world. No creature on earth shall defy him. But the evil will is still alive even in the followers of Christ, it still seeks to cut them off from fellowship with him; and that is why they must also pray that the will of God may prevail more and more in their hearts every day and break down all defiance" (Discipleship 166).

Psalm 40 echoes this theme -- "my delight is to do your will, O Lord!" -- and so may my heart and mind! Show me your way, O Lord; lead me in the path you have set out ahead of me. Again, Bonhoeffer speaks to the heart of the matter: "It is always true of the disciple that the spirit is willing but the flesh is weak, and he must therefore "watch and pray" (Discipleship 170).

December 30, 2010

Living to Teach Rather Than Teaching to Live

As I ponder the possibility of returning to teach at Handong University in Korea, I have been revisiting the Analects of Confucius. One in particular is especially applicable to anyone who senses that the calling upon their life is a call to teach. Of his own role as a teacher, Confucius said, "For anyone who brings even the smallest token of appreciation, I have yet to refuse instruction." This responsibility to the one seeking instruction was again impressed upon me when I read this morning these verses in The Wisdom of Solomon: "The beginning of wisdom is the most sincere desire for instruction, and concern for instruction is love of her." So when one is met with a request from those who are sincerely seeking instruction, the one who has a call to teach must give the most deliberate consideration to responding.

This type of thinking challenges me to confront the question: Do you teach to live or do you live to teach? Another way to put the question would be to examine whether I am accept the offer to teach primarily and principally as a means to make a living, or do I view the opportunity to teach as an open door through which God is directing me to proceed in faith depending upon him and him alone to provide for my earthly needs? Am I taking no thought for tomorrow, anxious over what I will eat or where I will live or how I will be clothed? Am I willing to follow on trusting the one who is my Guide, not only to make the way clear, but also to provide all that will be needed for me to progress along that way? Here Bonhoeffer instructs: "The only way to win assurance is by leaving to-morrow entirely in the hands of God and by receiving from him all we need for to-day" (Discipleship, 178).

Third Year

14

February 27, 2011

An Emerging Korean Call

Today marks my second full day back on the campus of Handong University in Pohang, Korea. When I departed from here last June, I expected to be coming back sometime in the future, but not so soon. I had returned to Missouri last summer first and foremost to be close to my mother whose health was failing. I also returned to resume my teaching position at Fontbonne and to continue PhD studies at Concordia Seminary, both in St. Louis. At that time, I believed that there would likely be a position opening on the full-time faculty at Fontbonne and the PhD studies were helping to bolster my credentials for that hoped-for appointment. In early November, however, I learned that the position would not be available and so, I suspended my graduate studies at the close of the fall quarter. Within days thereafter, my mother's health took a decided turn for the worse.

I spent most of December and January caring for my mother through three hospitalizations and intervening home convalescences. Earlier this month, Mom's time on earth drew to a close, and she entered her eternal rest on the 4th of February. Earlier in December, I had spoken to my mother about possibly returning to Handong and, even as her own health was fast fading, she was still encouraging me to respond to God's call.

My decision to return, though, did not come in an inspiring vision nor a challenging dream. Instead, it has been developing over the past eight years from my first meeting with Professors Lee Kukwoon and Lee Hee-eun at an academic conference in the fall of 2003 all the way through my months of service as a visiting professor just last year. It has been an emerging call that has, in turn, both gripped my heart and puzzled my mind. Having once again left behind in the States those who are most precious to me, I am, none the less, now more convinced than ever that this is the time and this is the place where I have been designed and equipped to serve others through the gifts God has given me. So I've come in response to what might aptly be described as my emerging Korean call. May God's sustaining grace keep and fortify me for each day. Classes start tomorrow!

March 1, 2011

A Good Place to Start -- Realizing Our End

I consider Prof. Richard Hughes a mentor though I've only met him twice -- once at a conference hosted by Baylor and a second time on the campus of Missouri Baptist University when he visited there as a part of the Rhodes Fellowship. In his book on the vocation of the Christian scholar, Hughes explains that he has one primary objective in every course he teaches -- to convince his students that they are going to die. I was vividly reminded of Hughes' principal objective yesterday when, in between my first day morning and afternoon classes, I attended the funeral of a 22-year old Handong student who had died while serving on mission trip last month in Israel. The student, Ms. Park, was one of a team of Handong students who were in Israel to work on a kibbutz. She died as a result of a tractor accident. It was her second mission trip to Israel.

As I sat in the funeral service and listened to the words of encouragement, comfort and hope offered by our campus pastor, I realized that this was the third funeral I had attended in the month of February. The first was my mother's. She had lived a very full and meaningful life that had even exceeded the "four score and ten" of Psalm 90:10 by nearly two years. Her funeral was a celebration of the reality of Christ's promise of resurrection and life in him. The second funeral was for a friend, Rodney -- the son of the Lutheran pastor who served the congregation where I grew up. I was confirmed under Rodney's father's instruction. Rodney had also been my family's life insurance agent and financial advisor. He died suddenly in middle-age of a rare brain disease. As a follower of Christ, though, he and his family had a settled trust in God's wise and good care. He peacefully yielded to his Lord's final call.

Then, within three days of my return to Korea, I was sitting in yet another funeral service -- this one, though, for a bright, energetic young person who had died at what most would readily say was the very beginning of her adult life. From the testimonies of her fellow students and her professors, Ms. Park had a devoted sense of mission and commitment to living her life for others. She was a psychology and counseling major at Handong and hoped to soon begin serving others as a counselor. Her sudden death has had a significant impact upon the Handong community. We have all been reminded of the brevity of life and the necessity of living each day to the fullest according the grace and calling of God. There is a tradition here in Korea that is practiced as a memorial to those who have died. A tree is planted to commemorate the person's life and a small memorial stone is placed near the newly planted tree.

This morning during my reflective walk about campus, I stopped by the memory tree that had been planted yesterday for Ms. Park. It is a beautiful 3-foot fir tree. It reminded me of three lives that had all been rooted in Christ and continue even now to bear fruit in the lives of others. May I be mindful each day of both the brevity of life and the certainty of death so that I might be living wholly and meaningfully today -- and, teach my students to do the same.

> *So teach us to number our days that we may get a heart of wisdom.* (Psalm 90:12)

March 5, 2011

What's That Beeping, Creeping That I Hear . . . ?
(With deepest apologies to E.A. Poe)

Once upon a midnight dreary, while I pondered, weak and weary,
Over many a quaint and curious volume of forgotten lore,
While I nodded, nearly sleeping, suddenly there came a beeping,
As of something gently creeping, creeping along my chamber floor.

No, I won't go any farther with this, but the beeping that pierced my nights for the past two days did nearly inspire a Homeric epic. That beeping, beeping, beeping continued nearly every five minutes through-out the entire night! What a way to be welcomed into your new apartment, though, I must say, the apartment that I've been provided this time is a great improvement over little (did I say little) studio apartment last year. What could it be? Was it the first faint taunts of a fire alarm or, maybe worse, a carbon-monoxide alarm that I had inadvertently activated by using the gas cook stove incorrectly? Was it coming from the radiant heating system that warms my floors? Was it my water heater? Had I forgotten to turn it off? I looked and looked, tried this and tried that, and I just couldn't get that beeping to STOP!

My only recourse was to go to bed and pack a pillow over my ears. Thankfully I was still so exhausted from the re-ordering of my circadian rhythm that I was able to sleep though the beeping, beeping -- at least for a few hours at a time. Yet, each time I awoke, I waiting anxiously, listening, hoping, and then the silence of the night was fractured again with that incessant BEEPING! I just can't go through another day with this beeping. I'll have to move into my office until I can get someone who knows how to make it stop. Or, is it just in my head? I'm I just imagining this or is it really real?? There's only one way for me to find out. The way that any good foreign faculty member at Handong begins his search for true knowledge.

I must call my TA! Now, as any regular reader of these postings might think, it would be a very difficult task for me to find someone who might have the potential to measure up to Mr. Mok. He was my most excellent TA who served me faithfully during my two semesters as a visiting professor here in 2009-2010. Now, upon my return to Handong, though, I did not have to look for a replacement -- for my new TA came to me. Ms. Han was the top student in my Legal Argumentation class last year. She also was the driving-force organizing and directing the Law & Advocacy study group with whom I served as a faculty sponsor. Over the past winter break, she and two other top law students from Handong traveled to the Netherlands for a research project at The Hague and the University of Utrecht. A more outstanding student I could not find if I had tried.

So, I placed a call to Ms. Han asking her to investigate the piercing beeping that was pervading my apartment. With just one short telephone call (in Korean) to the University's Housing Authority, she advised me that the beeping was a signal that the batteries powering the igniter for my gas stove top were soon to lose power and needed to be replaced. Amazing, all that needed to be done was to remove the old batteries from the back of my stove top (they were hidden back there) and replace them with new. Relief! No more beeping, beeping throughout the night. It is such a good thing to have an excellent TA!

March 8, 2011

May I Talk to You about My Next Step?

This is a question that is posed to me by my students several times a week. I've found that the typical Handong student is much more inclined to be thinking about her or his future than the run-of-the-mill student in the States. That's not to say, however, that I didn't have many exceptional students during my days of teaching at both Fontbonne and MBU who were quite serious about making their lives count. But, in general, I'm finding that the vast majority of students here think about making a difference in the world in the -- to borrow a phrase from Brother Bonhoeffer -- "the concrete realities of life in here and now." As a result, I've had many students visiting my office (on the 3d floor of All Nations Hall -- my window is the first one on the wing that extends off to the right of the corner tower), even within the first week of classes this semester, to talk about the plans they have made or are seeking to make for their studies and future roles of service.

Quite a number of them are interested in discussing whether the major in U.S. & International Law ("UIL") would help to equip them for positions in government or non-governmental organizations within their home countries or in developing third-world countries. In fact, just I was started composing this post yesterday afternoon, I had a knock on my office door and a freshman came in to discuss this very question. All freshman here at Handong start as "Global Studies" majors, and then within their first two semesters, they are required to declare two specific majors they wish to pursue through their studies. That's right, every student at Handong declares two majors! Many of the freshman are stopping by my office to discuss the UIL major.

Often, students will tell me of a personal "vision" they have for their lives. They describe the positions they imagine themselves occupying in leadership roles within major international corporations or political parties. Others have a strong commitment to developing countries and during their university studies use holiday breaks to work in Cambodia or Kyrgyzstan rather than travel to the sunny beaches of Phuket. In nearly every case, though, they have carefully thought through their plans and are looking ahead with very specific expectations. After recounting to me their plans and expectations, these students will then sit quietly with a slight smile on their faces as they await my comments. What should I say? Do I affirm their plans? Should I suggest alternatives? Should I encourage them or try to dissuade them for their proposed path, if I think it might be unwise? Because the Asian culture puts such a strong emphasis on young people respecting the advice and guidance of their elders, I'm put in quite a precarious position.

I don't have any fixed answers for them. I don't offer any formulas for success, nor do I try to tell them what God's will is for their lives. Instead, I feel like the Korean Buddhist monk, well-known for his silence and meditation, who when he was asked for a "word of wisdom" by his students told them, "Never trust the word of a monk." So rather than try to offer them specific counsel regarding their plans and choices, I encourage them to seek out the path where they can best serve the purpose to which they have been called. I suggest that success in life can only be found as we, individually and with others, seek to discover how we have been designed and equipped to serve others, and then start doing that service now in the midst of the concrete realities of life. Plans for the future can provide guidance for the way we live out today, but what is of even greater importance is living fully in the present -- making the most of each opportunity to serve that we are provided today.

> *"The mind of man plans his way, but the Lord directs his steps."* (Proverbs 16:9)

March 13, 2011

Two Weeks Into the New Semester

This weekend marks the completion of the first two weeks of the new semester. I feel like I've "hit the ground running," as we say back in the States. But, I need to be careful in choosing my phrases when speaking with my Korean colleagues and students. They tend to take each word quite literally. I'm not literally running. I'm not in that good of shape just yet. I am, though, doing quite a bit of walking. In fact, that is one of the prime factors that draws me to life at Handong. Here, I can live a walking-paced life. This morning, I walked to church, and later walked to lunch outside where I "helped" grill hot dogs and enjoyed a beautiful Spring-like afternoon with many who live on campus.

Each morning (or, nearly every morning), I get out and talk a walk-about. I head down road toward the main entrance and overlook the valley that stretches out between Handong's campus and the East Sea. If you look carefully at the picture above, you'll see the sea just beyond the rolling hills in the distance. I then make my way back up the long hill and around the road that circles the entire campus before returning to my apartment. The whole walk is nearly two miles. After preparing a breakfast of either fruit and cereal or -- on days when I'm a little more hungry -- French toast, scrambled eggs and bacon, I take another walk, much shorter though, over to All Nations Hall, and up to the third floor where my office is located. I usually arrive in time to check my email while listening to the latest news from St. Louis via KWMU's streaming audio on the web before making final preparations for my morning class.

After class, its back to the office for meetings with students and then off to lunch, usually with a colleague or two or on occasion, like this past Friday, I'll be invited to lunch by a group of students. There is a tradition here where students take their professors to lunch or dinner. It gives the students an opportunity to get to know their prof's in a more informal setting as well as being good practice with English conversation skills. Following lunch, an afternoon walk tends to keep my energy level up and helps to ward off the drowsiness that might otherwise tempt me back to my apartment for a little nap. Just a couple of days ago, I noticed another sure sign of spring when walking across campus. Some of the trees are already starting to blossom out.

Eventually, a whole host of cherry and pear trees across campus will be filled with delicate blossoms. Some will be white and others pink. It's an absolutely gorgeous sight! By then, I'll be walking even more since the temperatures will regularly be in the 60's and the rainy days of the late winter will have passed. The afternoons are filled with classes on Monday's and Thursday's, a faculty seminar on Wednesday's and a lively round table discussions with other international faculty on Friday's. My days are very full but not hectic. These first two weeks have begun to settle me in to a pattern and flow that I trust, by God's grace, will be both meaningful and productive as I seek to encourage my students to grow not only in knowledge but also in responsible service to others according to the callings on their lives.

March 16, 2011

There Arose a Reasoning Among Them ...

In every community of faith and learning there come times of conflict. Conflicts arise because these communities are composed of humans who are finite and fallen. At every university where I've taught over the past sixteen years there have been conflicts – conflicts between students and faculty members; between faculty and fellow faculty; and between faculty and university administration.

A university is in many respects like all other human communities that experience conflict from within among its members. Universities founded upon a common faith are no less prone to experience conflicts since, like every church fellowship, such a university is made-up of humans. So it should come as no surprise that a Christian university, especially one that is in its early years of growth and development, would experience conflict between some of its faculty and its administrative leaders.

Brother Bonhoeffer knew the reality of conflict from within a fellowship. During his days leading the Confessing Church's seminary at Finkenwalde, he experienced it. When he wrote about this experiment in Christian community in his little book Life Together, he began the fourth chapter with this warning:

> "'There arose a reasoning among them, which of them would be the greatest' (Luke 9:46). We know who it is that sows this thought in the Christian community. But perhaps we do not bear in mind enough that no Christian community ever comes together without this thought immediately emerging as a seed of discord. Thus at the very beginning of Christian fellowship there is engendered an invisible, often unconscious, life-and-death contest. 'There arose a reasoning among them'; this is enough to destroy a fellowship" (90).

Bonhoeffer's insight exposes the root cause for many, if not most, of these conflicts in our communities. It is the human desire for greatness or ascendancy over others. He continues,

> It is vitally necessary that every Christian community from the very outset face this dangerous enemy squarely, and eradicate it. There is not time to lose here, for from the first moment when a man meets another person he is looking for a strategic position he can assume and hold over against that person.

There are strong persons and weak ones. If a man is not strong, he immediately claims the right of the weak as his own and uses it against the strong. There are gifted and ungifted persons, simple people and difficult people, devout and less devout, the sociable and the solitary. Does not the ungifted person have to take up a position just as well as the gifted person, the difficult one as well as the simple? . . . Where is there a person who does not with instinctive sureness find the spot where he can stand and defend himself, but which he will never give up to another, for which he will fight with all the drive of his instinct of self-assertion?

All this can occur in the most polite or even pious environment. But the important thing is that a Christian community should know that somewhere in it there will certainly be 'a reasoning among them, which of them would be the greatest.' It is the struggle of the natural man for self-justification. He finds it only in comparing himself with others, in condemning and judging others. Self-justification and judging others go together, as justification by grace and serving others go together (91).

If this then is indeed the case, how may members of a community who are presently experiencing such conflict eradicate it? Bonhoeffer offers a potential path in the remainder of his chapter. There he addresses seven "ministries" that we owe to one another in community. Each bears upon me and my colleagues here at Handong if we would be peacemakers and ones who are committed to the growth of our community of learning into wholeness and mutual blessing that flows to all.

Those within our Handong community who would advance and seek to protect the students' "right to learn" owe the ministries Bonhoeffer commends to professors, students and fellow administrators. Those, on the other hand, who uphold and see to maintain the professors' "right to teach" likewise owe these ministries to all others within the community of learning. Rather than dispute over issues of control and authority, the ministries that Bonhoeffer teaches us to engage express avenues of service that lead toward mutual edification and the ultimate achievement of the goal of our community – the forming of whole persons who act responsibly in the service of others according to God's calling upon their lives.

The first of these ministries, as Bonhoeffer describes them, is "the ministry of holding one's tongue." "Often we combat our evil thoughts most effectively if we absolutely refuse to allow them to be expressed in words" (91). We are admonished in Scripture to be "slow to speak" (James 1:19), so we would do well to hold our tongue and think thoroughly we express comments, especially when they are criticisms of others. Bonhoeffer advises that "where this discipline of the tongue is practiced right from the beginning, each individual will make a matchless discovery. He will be able to cease from constantly scrutinizing the other person, judging him, condemning him, putting him in his particular place where he can gain ascendancy over him and thus doing violence to him as a person. Now he can allow the brother to exist as a completely free person, as God made him to be" (92-93).

The second ministry is meekness. "He who would learn to serve must first learn to think little of himself" (94). This is not self-loathing, but rather a proper view of self. "Only he who lives by the forgiveness of his sin in Jesus Christ will rightly think little of himself" (95). Such a perspective, Bonhoeffer acknowledges, leads to a challenging conclusion: "To forego self-conceit and to associate with the lowly means . . . to consider oneself the greatest of sinners. . . If my sinfulness appears to me to be in any way smaller or less detestable in comparison with the sins of others, I am still not recognizing my sinfulness at all. . . He who would serve his brother in the fellowship must sink all the way down to these depths of humility" (96).

Holding one's tongue and meekness lead naturally to the third ministry we owe one another in community – that of listening. "Just as love to God begins with listening to His Word, so the beginning of love for the brethren [i.e. for others] is learning to listen to them" (97). To be an effective listener, though, is a skill we must be devoted to developing. Our tendency is merely to "wait to talk" when in conversation with others. What we need to be doing is authentic listening. Bonhoeffer warns that "he who can no longer listen to his brother will soon be no longer listening to God either; he will be doing nothing but prattle in the presence of God" (98).

By listening we are enabled to understand the needs of others and so reach out to them with the ministry of helpfulness. "This means, initially, simple assistance in trifling, external matters . . . Nobody is too good for the meanest (i.e. lowest) service. One who worries about the loss of time that such petty, outward acts of helpfulness entail is usually taking the importance of his own career too solemnly" (99).

The next service we owe is the ministry of bearing. "'Bear ye one another's burdens, and so fulfill the law of Christ' (Gal. 6:2). . . Bearing means forbearing and sustaining. . . The Christian . . . must bear the burden of a brother. He must suffer and endure the brother. It is only when he is a burden that another person is really a brother and not merely an object to be manipulated" (100). As we extend this service, Bonhoeffer calls us to bear both the freedom of the other person as well as his sin through regularly practicing forgiveness.

The thoughtful engagement of these first five ministries – holding one's tongue, meekness, listening, helpfulness and bearing – provides the only sure foundation for the next – the ministry of proclaiming the Word. This ministry is not the "preaching of the

Word" but rather "that unique situation in which one person bears witness in human words to another person, bespeaking the whole consolation of God, the admonition, the kindness, and the severity of God" (103-104). "We speak to one another on the basis of the help we both need. We admonish one another to go the way that Christ bids us to go. We warn one another against the disobedience that is our common destruction" (106).

Bonhoeffer concludes with the ultimate service we owe -- the ministry of authority. This ministry, however, can only be exercised by those who have first fulfilled the all that come before it because "Jesus made authority in the fellowship dependent upon brotherly service" (108). "Every cult of personality that emphasizes the distinguished qualities, virtues, and talents of another person, even though these be of an altogether spiritual nature, is worldly and has no place in the Christian community . . . The Church does not need brilliant personalities but faithful servants of Jesus and the brethren" (108-109).

Indeed, no community of faith, no community of learning, needs brilliant personalities. What we need are faithful followers of Christ who seek daily, by His grace, to serve one another according to the call of God. What is needed to eradicate the attitudes and actions that destroy our community of learning are men and women possessed with the mind of Christ that seeks not their own interests and rights but those of others. Such an approach to sustaining our community of learning and faith will not pit the right to learn against the right to teach. Rather, it will serve others by taking seriously the responsibility to teach and the responsibility to learn as we seek together to obey the call of Christ and serve the needs of others in the here and now.

March 17, 2011

The Breastplate of St. Patrick

I bind unto myself today
The strong Name of the Trinity,
By invocation of the same,
The Three in One and One in Three.

I bind this day to me for ever.
By power of faith, Christ's incarnation;
His baptism in the Jordan river;
His death on Cross for my salvation;
His bursting from the spicèd tomb;
His riding up the heavenly way;
His coming at the day of doom;*

I bind unto myself today.
I bind unto myself the power
Of the great love of the cherubim;
The sweet 'well done' in judgment hour,
The service of the seraphim,
Confessors' faith, Apostles' word,
The Patriarchs' prayers, the Prophets' scrolls,
All good deeds done unto the Lord,
And purity of virgin souls.

I bind unto myself today
The virtues of the starlit heaven,
The glorious sun's life-giving ray,
The whiteness of the moon at even,
The flashing of the lightning free,
The whirling wind's tempestuous shocks,
The stable earth, the deep salt sea,
Around the old eternal rocks.

I bind unto myself today
The power of God to hold and lead,
His eye to watch, His might to stay,
His ear to hearken to my need.
The wisdom of my God to teach,
His hand to guide, His shield to ward,
The word of God to give me speech,
His heavenly host to be my guard.

Against the demon snares of sin,
The vice that gives temptation force,
The natural lusts that war within,
The hostile men that mar my course;
Or few or many, far or nigh,
In every place and in all hours,
Against their fierce hostility,
I bind to me these holy powers.

Against all Satan's spells and wiles,
Against false words of heresy,
Against the knowledge that defiles,
Against the heart's idolatry,
Against the wizard's evil craft,
Against the death wound and the burning,
The choking wave and the poisoned shaft,
Protect me, Christ, till Thy returning.

Christ be with me, Christ within me,
Christ behind me, Christ before me,
Christ beside me, Christ to win me,
Christ to comfort and restore me.
Christ beneath me, Christ above me,
Christ in quiet, Christ in danger,
Christ in hearts of all that love me,
Christ in mouth of friend and stranger.

I bind unto myself the Name,
The strong Name of the Trinity;
By invocation of the same.
The Three in One, and One in Three,
Of Whom all nature hath creation,
Eternal Father, Spirit, Word:
Praise to the Lord of my salvation,
Salvation is of Christ the Lord.

March 18, 2011

They Could Not Keep Their Eyes Open

During my morning readings a few days back, I came across this phrase. It suddenly dawned upon me that Jesus' students encountered the very same struggles that students today face. At one of the most important times in their life, when they had been asked specifically by their teacher to stay alert, they were found falling asleep! And we're not talking about one of the stragglers at the back of the class. No, these were Jesus' three top students -- the inner circle -- the creme of the crop -- the "summa cum laude" guys -- who couldn't keep their eyes open!

So, if that was the case with Peter, James and John, this poor teacher should not be surprised nor offended when even some of his most diligent students occasionally can't seem to keep their eyes open during class. Now, I try to provide some incentive for them to stay awake. Rather than standing in one place at the front of the classroom (which I have observed seems to be the norm among many of the local prof's here), I try to infuse some variety into the discussion by walking about through the aisles and even sometimes taking a place at the back of the room in order to challenge the students to adjust to a new posture in order to engage a new perspective.

In addition to these peripatetic tendencies, I also take some pains to restrain my natural inclination to speak up and so try to lower my volume a bit. As you might imagine, though, this strategy tends to have the opposite effect than the one I'm seeking. So, those short periods of soft tones are usually followed by an abrupt exclamation or the invocation of some Latin maxim whether it is application to the legal issue under consideration or not. But you might be asking at this point, why is it that my students are having such a struggle to stay awake. Am I that boring??? Well --- I'll let you ask my students to answer that one. I will only say that I'm trying to be ever interesting and engaging. I'm trying to talk less and ask questions more -- to encourage dialogue and eliminate monologue. That said, though, there is another possible cause. You see, students here are very conscientious about their studies that they will often stay up quite late diligently studying in preparation for the next day's classes. They study so much, that when they come to class, the struggle to stay awake -- not because they're uninterested in the subject under discussion or just bored -- they're EXHAUSTED!

Since that is indeed most often the case, I just might start bringing a couple extra pillows to my classes and offer them as rewards (not to be used during lectures, however!) to the most diligent disciple who, like Peter, James & John, find that they "could not keep their eyes open."

March 24, 2011

Truth is Truth whether from Lips of . . .

I look to C.S. Lewis as one of my model teachers. The portrayal of Lewis' tutorial with his students in the film, Shadowlands, is one of the finest displays of formation-in-process that I can point to in contemporary culture. He challenges his students to explore the significance of a rose as a metaphor for desire. Through a series of questions, he guides his students to ponder a persistent question: "What is desire's one essential quality?" When one of his pupils shrugs-off the answer proposed, Lewis exhorts him into a deeper debate. The student though, at this early point in their relationship, is reticent to take up the gauntlet.

Now, I don't know if Anthony Hopkins' Lewis is an accurate portrayal, but it is an authentically inspiring one to me, and I think it is quite consistent with the Lewis we come to know in his books, especially Mere Christianity and his essays contained in God in the

Dock. Lewis' thinking (and his teaching, I would imagine) was significantly formed by the works of the Scottish pastor and novelist George MacDonald. One of the books by Lewis I ever purchased after reading The Screwtape Letters in my high school years was a little paperback entitled, George MacDonald: Anthology. In the preface to this collection, Lewis wrote: "In making these extracts, I have been concerned with MacDonald not as a writer but as a Christian teacher" (14).

Though he had never met MacDonald, Lewis recounts how his works and life, as told by MacDonald's son in the biography he wrote of his father, substantially shaped his approach to writing and to living. One of the most telling quotes that Lewis includes among the 365 extracts (most coming from MacDonald's sermons) composing this little volume is this: "Truth is truth, whether from the lips of Jesus or Balaam" (27). From the very first time I read that line nearly 35 years ago it was indelibly impressed upon my thinking. MacDonald's words have continued challenged me to listen carefully to many speakers, to read thoughtfully many authors, and to watch observantly many actors.

The search for truth -- true truth, as Francis Schaeffer has called it -- will take us in a variety of directions. I was reminded of this just last evening. As on nearly every Wednesday evening, I was engaged in a discussion of the Scriptures with some of my fellow colleagues here at Handong. Our focus was the first chapter of James, and someone pointed out how this passage emphasizes the need to look into the Scriptures as a mirror that can reveal to us our true selves. This comment led another participant in the study to mention a book entitled The Man in the Mirror. When I heard that phrase, my thoughts turned to a pop song with the same title from the 80's by Michael Jackson.

And being the sort of "quick to speak" guy that I am, I told the group that Jackson had written a song about the "man in the mirror." The mention of the "king of pop's" name must have struck a dissonant chord though, because another of my colleagues promptly declared, "But Michael Jackson got it wrong!" I replied, "Did he? Didn't he just express what Gandhi had said -- "Become the change you wish to make in the world"? Well, my mention of Michael Jackson and Gandhi in the same sentence seemed to be quite enough to alert the group's leader that we (read "I") had now gone way too far afield in our discussion. It was a Bible study for heaven's sake!

But hold on! Truth is truth, right? Whether spoken from the lips of Jesus or Balaam, right? Whether spoken from the lips of Gandhi or sung by Michael Jackson? -- Well you tell me. Did Jackson get it right or not? Here's what he sings:

"As I, Turn Up The Collar On My
Favorite Winter Coat
This Wind Is Blowin' My Mind
I See The Kids In The Street,
With Not Enough To Eat
Who Am I, To Be Blind?
Pretending Not To See Their Needs
"A Summer's Disregard,
A Broken Bottle Top
And A One Man's Soul
They Follow Each Other On
The Wind Ya' Know
'Cause They Got Nowhere To Go
That's Why I Want You To Know

"I'm Starting With The Man In The Mirror
I'm Asking Him To Change His Ways
And No Message Could Have Been Any Clearer
If You Wanna Make The World A Better Place
Take A Look At Yourself,
And Then Make A Change.

"I've Been A Victim Of A Selfish Kind Of Love
It's Time That I Realize
That There Are Some With No Home,
Not A Nickel To Loan
Could It Be Really Me,
Pretending That They're Not Alone?
"A Willow Deeply Scarred,
Somebody's Broken Heart
And A Washed-Out Dream
They Follow The Pattern Of The Wind, Ya' See
Cause They Got No Place To Be
That's Why I'm Starting With Me

"I'm Starting With The Man In The Mirror
I'm Asking Him To Change His Ways
And No Message Could Have Been Any Clearer
If You Wanna Make The World A Better Place
Take A Look At Yourself,
And Then Make A Change."

That's what Michael Jackson sang. Here's what James wrote:

> *But be doers of the word, and not hearers only, deceiving yourselves. For if anyone is a hearer of the word and not a doer, he is like a man who looks intently at his natural face in a mirror. For he looks at himself and goes away and at once forgets what he was like. But the one who looks into the perfect law, the law of liberty, and perseveres, being no hearer who forgets but a doer who acts, he will be blessed in his doing.* (James 1:22-25)

If truth is truth no matter from whose lips the message is spoken or from whose pen the words are written, then it would appear to me that a question of first importance is indeed: Have I made a change in my life?

March 29, 2011

A Most Delightful Place, A Sacred Place, My Favorite Place!

Do you have a favorite place? A place that you would go if you had the opportunity? A place that brings you joy? A place of delight? A place that brings you refreshment? When my wife Sandy and I first began traveling abroad in the summer of 2001, we tagged along on a mission trip sponsored by Missouri Baptist University where I had been teaching, by that time, for a number of years. We traveled to England and spent two delightful weeks doing physical labor as we worked on the rehab of a 16th century manor house that had been transformed into a youth camping center. That place -- The Oakes -- became one of my first favorite places.

Sandy and I were able to return there in May of 2004 and see first-hand the on-going development and growth of a wonderful community led our good friends, Dan & Billie Thaw. We experienced a true sense of joy as we visited the Oakes and met even more people who were continuing to contribute to its renewal. It has become a special place where the light of truth is being shared with many young people from across the entire United Kingdom. On that same visit to the UK, Sandy and I were also able to travel to Ireland for the first time. There we spent a delightful time touring in Dublin, Bray and the surrounding Counties. One place, though, completely captured me.

It became my favorite place in all of Ireland (granted, I have been everywhere in Ireland, but I'm quite confident that this place will be hard to beat if I ever get back to the Emerald Isle). The place is called Glendalough -- the valley between the two lakes. It is the site of an early Celtic Christian community founded by St. Kevin, who lived in the generation just after Patrick.

Later during this tour of the UK, Sandy and I were invited to visit friends in Brecon, Wales. Our hosts took us out for a day of sightseeing in the South of Wales. We drove along the Wye River Valley and came upon one of the most sacred sites in all of Wales -- Tintern Abbey. It was just above and overlooking this Abbey that Woodsworth wrote his "Few Lines . . ." My heart had been captured my yet another special place.

Though the Oakes, Glendalough and Tintern Abbey remain my favorite places in England, Ireland, and Wales, my fondness for them has, I must confess, grown somewhat dimmer these days. Having now returned to the East, one place in all of Korea has become and I'm sure will continue to remain, my most favorite of all. I first visited this place in July of 2004 when the students who were taking my short summer course at Handong International Law School (HILS) suggested that we take a break from our studies and enjoy a Saturday touring sights in a nearby town.

They drove me to Gyeongju -- the ancient capital of Korea -- and then up the mountains surrounding Gyeongju to a place called "Bulguksa" -- a Buddhist monastery. The experience I sensed upon walking up to the central structures of this place was much like the feeling I had had at Glendalough and Tintern Abbey -- I knew that I was venturing upon a sacred place. Interestingly, Bulguksa's founding dates back to about the same time as the founding of Glendalough -- around the 8th century. This past weekend, I had the privilege of making my fourth visit to Bulguksa. Each time I've been there, I've seen something new. This time I paused along a path and looked back toward the main stairway that leads up to the central worship area. I took the picture you see here.

On my three previous visits, I followed the guide book and stopped at a point well to the far west of this main stairway. This is the perspective you see in all the photo's. Its a beautiful sight, no doubt (just take a look below), but I now realize that this view does not convey the fullest sense of the beauty of Bulguksa -- the beauty that shines as you see how the structures built there are so carefully balanced with the surrounding natural setting. I had unknowingly limited my perspective by just looking from the well-known perspective. What I needed to do was to look at things from a new perspective. When I did, the wonder and beauty of this place only expanded in my mind. It has become my favorite place in all of Korea in a new way. The early blossoms of Spring hint at a coming beauty that will explode across the hillsides as more and more of the cherry trees bloom.

As you walk along the paths that lead you through the grounds, the delight and beauty of this place only become more and more apparent. Each time I visit, my spirit is lifted and I feel a sense of refreshment that is much more that just what comes from a vigorous walk on a brisk day. It is more than a physical rejuvenation, it is truly soul sustenance. In fact, it is difficult to put it into words, because words in themselves seem a too limited means of conveying what the whole of my person experiences in this place. Simply put, it is now my favorite place. I can't wait to go back!

15

April 2, 2011

Playing the Fool . . . and Teaching, too

I'm always trying to engage my students through new approaches that I hope will prompt them to examine different perspectives on the persistent questions of life. So, this past Friday I thought I might take a slightly different approach to April Fool's Day. I came to class dressed in a brown Franciscan-like habit and without my glasses or shoes (and sockless, too!). To say my students were taken aback would be putting it somewhat mildly. Now, you have to understand that in Asian culture in general (and Korean culture in particular), students are taught to accept what their teachers present to them. That being said, many were still trying hard to suppress their laughter. Has professor gone completely crazy? Has separation from his wife and family driven him mad? Does he really think that he has become a monk?

None of those questions were expressly stated, but you can be sure most of them were puzzling more than one student's mind. So what was the point of this first of April performance? I wanted to do for my new students at Handong what I had first done for students at Missouri Baptist University seven years ago on another April fool's Day. In the attire of a follower of Francis of Assisi, I told them his story and how he came to be known as Francis the Fool.

I had been assigned the responsibility of giving the message for the student chapel service at MBU on the first of April. Earlier that year, I had read G.K. Chesterton's Life of St. Francis. Chesterton's portrayal of Francis challenged me to think more deeply about what it means to follow Jesus fully. Francis sought to live as Jesus lived and to love as Jesus loved. He reached out and touched the leper just as Christ had done. He left behind the wealth and security offered him by his family in order to find the fullness of life as he took seriously Christ's teaching to consider the birds of the air and the flowers of the field.

Having been so challenged by Francis' life, it was quite obvious to me that I was meant to tell his story in that chapel service on the first of April seven years ago. I thought it would make a more memorable impression if I told the story as Francis himself. So, now here at Handong, I wanted to continue the tradition and pass along the lessons from the life of the one who was called "Francis the Fool" -- a name that I'm sure he did not resent since he was seeking to follow the one who many had regarded as "God's own Fool." Evidently that chapel message seven years ago was memorable. When one of my Handong student's posted a picture to Facebook during our Friday morning class, one of my former students from MBU, who was on-line at the time, commented within minutes: "I remember that robe!" I guess, playing the fool can sometimes be an effective means of teaching.

April 19, 2011

If I Stand, Let Me Stand Upon the Promise . . .

Something dawned on me the other week. Actually, it has hit me like a ton of bricks! I'm at Handong this semester teaching without Sandy. She's back in the States continuing her nursing studies -- and doing quite well in them, I might add. When we thought about me returning to teach here this semester, we thought that I could once again make it through a semester even though we would be separated by half a world's distance. That expectation was based upon the fact that I've done it before. In 2009, I taught here for a semester while Sandy was still back in St. Louis. When I returned over the Christmas break that year, Sandy then joined in our return to Handong for the new semester that began in February 2010. But, there is a big difference now. Why it hadn't struck me before, I will never know. But, I know the difference now. My first semester's hermitage here at Handong in 2009 was during a Fall term. This time I'm here in hermitage during the Spring! You know, that time of the year when trees blossom, flowers bloom and birds begin to sing. On top of the seasonal impact, there are also the many vivid memories of times Sandy and I spent just one short year ago exploring the Korean countryside and culture together. Consequently, I find myself "longing for my home" a whole lot more these days than ever before while I've been here.

When I get into one of these increasingly more frequently-occurring "down" times, I have resorted to listening to my favorite musicians as a means of encouragement and comfort. One particular concert given by Rich Mullins and his band back in the late 1990's is available in its entirety on YouTube. His songs have become favorites and reliable sources of strength in these days when physical weariness only compounds a deeper psychological and spiritual disheartenedness (if that is even a word). Here's one of Rich Mullins' songs that has been a special blessing to my soul during these cloudy days. "If I stand, let me stand on the promise that You will pull me through. and if I weep, let me weep as a man who is longing for his home."

Blessed be the God and Father of our Lord Jesus Christ! According to his great mercy, he has caused us to be born again to a living hope through the resurrection of Jesus Christ from the dead, to an inheritance that is imperishable, undefiled, and unfading, kept in heaven for you, who by God's power are being guarded through faith for a salvation ready to be revealed in the last time.

> *In this you rejoice, though now for a little while, if necessary, you have been grieved by various trials, so that the tested genuineness of your faith—more precious than gold that perishes though it is tested by fire—may be found to result in praise and glory and honor at the revelation of Jesus Christ. Though you have not seen him, you love him. Though you do not now see him, you believe in him and rejoice with joy that is inexpressible and filled with glory.* (1 Peter 1:3-8)

April 21, 2011

What a Wonder a Walk Can Be . . . When Only We Open Our Eyes and Look Up!

Ordinarily on Thursday's my lunch hour is spent with faculty colleagues, but this week's midterm exams prompted the cancellation of our regular departmental meeting. I was delighted, then, to receive an invitation to join two of my best students for a relaxing lunch on the patio of the campus restaurant. We sat outside to enjoy the sunshine and the increasingly warmer temperatures that have finally started to make their way to the eastern coast of Korea -- a bit later this spring than usual, I am told.

As our lunch progressed, though, the wind started to pick-up and even blew some exam review papers from the books on our table. I had to make a quick dash to dab them before another gust took them over the wall and into the woods. It also started to get a bit darker as some clouds rolled-in. Today's forecast is calling for rain tomorrow, but it appeared now to be on its way to making an earlier arrival.

Following lunch, one of my students accompanied me on a walk back across campus. We continued the conversation from our time around the table as we walked. Then, all of a sudden, she stopped and said, "Professor, look up!" As I did, I saw what can only be described as a broad brush stroke of blazing color across the clouds. It wasn't a rainbow. Yet, the full spectrum of light, from violet through every hue to red, was flowing over the clouds that had gathered above. We were both stopped flat-footed, awestruck. It was as if the Aurora Borealis were dancing in the midday sky. As we stood gazing into the heavens, a few other students came walking by. Some passed by without a pause, but a few wondered what we were looking at. As they turned and looked-up, their mouths dropped open. What a sight! And, it didn't disappear in a few moments. It lingered as the clouds moved slowly across the sky. This "floating rainbow" stretched out its waves of brilliance. Had I stayed in my office today and done what I ordinarily do -- focused my view on what is below -- the demands of the day -- I would have entirely missed the beauty that was shining above. I'm thankful I was invited to take a walk. I'm thankful I was urged to open my eyes and look-up!

In one of his most precious songs, Michael Card sings to his children and tells them of his prayers -- a father's longing for his children to see increasingly the wonder of life that will bring the sunrise of their smile.

Now close your eyes so you can see,
Your own unfinished memories,
Now open them, for time is brief,
And you'll be blest beyond belief,

Now glance above you at the sky,
There's beauty there to blind the eye,
I ask all this then wait awhile,
To see the dawning of your smile.

Looking ahead to Easter morning's sunrise, may I always be reminded to glance above me at the sky!

> *If then you have been raised with Christ, seek the things that are above, where Christ is, seated at the right hand of God. Set your minds on things that are above, not on things that are on earth. For you have died, and your life is hidden with Christ in God. When Christ who is your life appears, then you also will appear with him in glory.* (Colossians 3:14)

May 7, 2011

Living More AND Less

I wrote this brief piece about ten years ago. I am recently finding, though, that I need to take heed to the following "suggestions" even more so during my life abroad this semester @ Handong ~

A common reply to the everyday question "How are you doing?" is often, "Well...okay...more or less." Most of us find our day-to-day lives to be somewhere in between the "more" and the "less" of health and wellness, spiritual wholeness and, if we are honest, mental sane-ness. May I then make a few humble suggestions to encourage us all to live "more and less" as a means of growing beyond the "more or less" of life?

I offer these as suggestions, not reproofs. I readily admit that the biggest beam resides in my own eye as I regularly fail the more's and much too often practice the less's. To some, they may seem trite and clichéd, but I trust to others they may prove helpful in some small way. With that said, may we all be living by doing . . .

More Reading, Less Watching
Good books are a treasure. Search them out!
TV (films, the web) can be a trap. Watch, above all, your step.

More Listening, Less Talking
Do I really listen?
Or, just wait to talk?

More Walking, Less Sitting
What wondrous things we can see and ideas ponder on a daily walk!
But, oh how stresses seem to weigh us down as we sit.

More Drinking, Less Eating
Water, that is. Cool, clear water!
Food, yes, food. Start by reducing portions.

More Helping, Less Hounding
"How may I help you?" is a wonderful way to encourage someone.
"What can you do for me?" is an attitude that often prompts us to pound someone.

More Asking, Less Accusing
Seek to understand before expecting to be understood.
Attribute the best motives to others, rather than accuse them of the worst.

More Giving, Less Keeping
Remember Jesus said that you will be happier by giving than by expecting to get. The less things we hold on to, the less hold things have on us.

More Thanking, Less Expecting
In everything give thanks, for this is God's will for you.
The way we thank others reveals whether we truly thank God.
So, see the acts of others as their gifts to you, not as efforts to fulfill your expectations.

More Singing, Less Sighing

When a song is first in our heart, then it authentically resounds in our voice. Sighing, however, is a true downer wherever it resides.

More Conserving, Less Consuming
The good things in life are few – they are to be savored.
The fast things in life are plenty – they favor by fattening.

More Serving, Less Summonsing
Jesus summed-up his life's purpose in the words: "to serve and to give." Don't expect someone to wash your feet; take up the basin and the towel – today.

May 10, 2011

My Korean Birthday . . . Quite an Auspicious Day!!

What can I say? I think Sandy put it best in her email to me, "Koreans really know how to celebrate!" And so began the celebrations this past week on Tuesday evening with a "Pre-Birthday Pizza Party" @ one of my students' favorite spots -- "Mr. Pizza" That's a Hawaiian Special with the candles atop it in front of me. After enjoying our pizza and endless salad bar feast (the true attraction here -- all you can eat salads!!), we played a hilarious game of "Pictionary" using words and phrases from the case these Law & Advocacy students are preparing for Mock Trial in a couple of weeks. So, what picture would you draw if the phrase you were given was "in loco parentis"? But, the celebrations didn't end there, even though that would have been an amazingly fabulous time. No, from Mr. Pizza we all walked down the stroll through Yukguri (the downtown shopping and entertainment district) to what you in the States would call a karaoke club, but what is here called a noraebang (singing room). That's right, each group that comes in gets its own room equipped with an amazing karaoke machine housing literally tens of thousands of favorite songs from all generations and genres! I'm told this is the number one form of party entertainment in Korea. I was happy to join right in. It was my birthday, right?? Well, pre-birthday, at least!! Ms. YeEun Han, Mr. Vu and I crooned "My Heart Will Go On" together. What a blast!

The pre-birthday party was so overwhelming that I had to take a day of rest on Wednesday! Several students stopped by my office during the day, though, to drop off wonderful little gifts and cards. One, Ms. Ha, even presented me with some home-made rich dark chocolates!! Couldn't even eat half a bite without a glass of milk!! Amazing! Another student, Ms. Grimi Kim, brought me two small cactus plants for my office. Each gift was accompanied with a beautiful card containing more than just the ordinary "Happy Birthday" wishes you find on American cards. Every card conveyed a hand-written expression of good wishes and prayers. Then, about 9:30 Wednesday evening I received a call from Ms. Shin, the president of our Law & Advocacy study group asking if she and another student might drop-off "something" at my apartment later on that evening.

"Later on" turned-out to be nearly 11:30pm and the two students turned into over a dozen carrying with them a cake, presents and a large decorated envelope full of birthday cards. They sang the "Happy Birthday" song twice as the midnight hour approached, and we all enjoyed pieces of the delicious cake. At the stroke of the new day, they all became the very first to wish me "Happy Birthday" on the Fifth of May! What amazing students I have!! Their presents included a beautiful orchid plant for my office and a jar of hard candies that one very special and perceptive student had noticed I particularly enjoy. They do not miss a beat!! When I started to open their cards, though, everyone said that I should wait until after they left. I think they knew that when I read them I might very likely start crying. And, after they did all depart around 12:30, I read them all and I did. So now, I have been given a "pre-birthday" party and a strike-of-midnight birthday party, but the celebrations are, in fact, still just beginning. On the morning of the fifth, I awoke to a beautiful day and took my regular break-of-dawn walkabout campus and was serenaded by some of the most unusual bird songs I have yet to hear here in Korea. Could it have been that my birthday made me a bit more attentive to their tunes??

By eight, I was seated on the sidelines of the soccer field with students and fellow colleagues to watch our Law Department men engage the Engineering Department on the pitch. Unfortunately, our men could not engineer a sufficient number of successful shots on goal, and this one went into the books with disappointment. It was, though, a hard fought match, and after all, that is what we are daily called to give! At eleven, I joined with my dear friends from the Pohang International Community core group and we journeyed the short distance from campus to Chilpo Beach, and what a beach party it was!! We cooked-out and enjoyed a great meal together with the sea breeze blowing in our hair and the sun beaming down on us!

Pastor Richie's son, Joseph, presented me with one of my most precious birthday gifts -- an original picture drawn and colored by Joseph to remind me of our day at the sea. (It has now been posted to a prominent spot on my refrigerator). I even tried to convince Richie that it was a great day to join me in taking a swim in the ocean, but my powers of persuasion were not (fortunately for him and me) sufficiently potent on this occasion. But wait, ... it was my birthday!!! . . . . don't I get to do what I want to do on my birthday??? Rest easy Sandy! I didn't end up going swimming, but I did have a thoroughly good time with the best of friends on an amazingly beautiful day at the beach!! I even jumped for joy!! Thanks, Boyeon, for convincing me that I could!!

And, you might think the celebrations had reached their zenith, but you would be wrong!! We're not done yet!! After returning to campus, cleaning off and out the sand I brought back in my clothes and on my legs and feet, I enjoyed a nap. Well, it was my birthday, right! I had to rest because I was due to meet my TA, Ms. Juyoun Han, and three other students for a birthday dinner at Hyoam Restaurant -- the nicest restaurant on campus.

While it was much more reserved and definitely less rowdy (for Ms. Han would have no other way) than my midday celebration at the beach, we did enjoy our fair share of laughs as I tried to give Daniel and Hojong, who are now both law students at Handong International Law School, some pointers on wooing women. I don't think they thought my idea of a first-date walk in the cemetery was all that helpful, though. Yet, they could not dispute that it at least worked for me. Just goes to show you how loving and caring my dearest Sandy was and continues to be! So, as Daniel practiced his French to himself ("mon chéri amour"), Hojong wasted no time in getting closer to one of the fairest young ladies on campus, Ms. Shin, who had also joined in my celebratory dinner.

At the end of the dinner, the four disappeared for a few minutes only to return with a birthday cheesecake adorned with several candles less than 52 -- they would have needed special permission from the fire marshal for that! It topped-off an amazingly fun and delightful evening. But wait, there's still more . . . . After departing Hyoam, we walked across campus to the playing field to cheer on our Law Department girls' wild horse team in their match against the Design Department. Wild horse is a game combining the intensity of American football, the speed and agility of soccer and the ruggedness of rugby (sometimes). The team presented me with a great present -- a thoroughly decisive victory! Go Law!!
So that was it! I barely made it back to my campus apartment before collapsing! Although completely exhausted as I was, I couldn't have been happier to have enjoyed such an auspicious day! Sandy was indeed right: Koreans really do know how to celebrate! I only wish she could have been here to join in on all the fun!

16

June 14, 2011

Campaign for a Balanced Life

I've undertaken a campaign. It is not a political one, nor is it military, nor even a campaign for social or economic justice. Each of those may very well have their own time and place and possibly an appropriate demand for my attention, but the campaign that has gripped me especially during these last weeks of the semester here at Handong is a campaign for living a more balance life.

The busy-ness of life, especially in the life of students and professors alike, has been advancing with menacing force over this past month. The campaign I have undertaken is my small attempt to thwart this advance. And how might you ask am I mounting such a campaign? What tactics and strategies am I employing? My chief weapon is the camera function on my mobile phone, and my subjects are the flowers of the field.

As I walk about campus each morning, I purposefully search out beauty -- the beauty Jesus taught us to behold when he said, "Consider the lilies." When I find beauty, I photograph it. And then as I go about my day, I display the photo I have most recently taken on my mobile's wallpaper and simply ask the student or professor I have encountered along the way whether they know where on campus this object of beauty may be seen, and when seen considered.

If they know, they have already joined the ranks of my campaign. If they're willing to search it out, they are well on their way. If, though, they do not know nor care to discover, then they have been overcome by our common enemy -- the tyranny of the urgent. I seek to persuade them that a life balanced with the pursuit and appreciation of beauty might actually enhance their performance of those duties that they seem so burdened to fulfill. It might just help to lift that burden that has so captured their attention that all around them seems a haze or what's worst, a grayness. Some flowers, however, have caught the gaze of eyes that have been graciously opened by the belief that one thing is necessary and when we choose it, we will have chosen the better part of life -- a more balanced life.

> *Consider the lilies of the field, how they grow: they neither toil nor spin, yet I tell you, even Solomon in all his glory was not arrayed like one of these.*

August 19, 2011

"Absence Makes the Heart Grow Fonder"

According to one source, the Roman poet Sextus Propertius gave us the earliest form of this saying in his Elegies: "Always toward absent lovers, love's tide stronger flows." Personally, I thought it must have been Shakespeare or Guillaume de Lorris, but no matter. Is it true? Does spatial separation deepen authentic love? And if so, does the greater the distance and longer the time of separation prompt an even deeper devotion? I do believe it does, and I say this not just as an intellectual contention or an emotional aspiration, but rather, based upon lived-experience. On the 26th of August, my wife and I will celebrate the 33d anniversary of our marriage. We will, however, be half-a-world away from one another. Sandy is in St. Louis, and me here, once again, at

Handong. But in the truest sense, only space separates us. I've just returned to begin preparations for another semester's teaching this fall. The wonderful seven weeks of our time together this summer during my leave in the States passed all too quickly, but it did afford delightful times of refreshment and strengthening of our relationship. Now, I'm looking ahead to the third semester that I will be here teaching in the absence of my Beloved. But periods of separation from family are not uncommon in these present times. Last semester, Sandy would often remind me during our Skype calls that the men and women who serve us so faithfully in the military are frequently duty-bound to lengthy times of separation from their loved ones.

When country calls, soldiers and sailors obey. Would it be any less the duty of a follower of Christ to heed his command even though it meant parting from loved-ones for that time of service? Jesus has promised his followers this: *"Truly, I say to you, there is no one who has left house or wife or brothers or parents or children, for the sake of the kingdom of God, who will not receive many times more in this time, and in the age to come eternal life."* (Luke 18:29-30). But he gives more grace, and by God's grace and mercy, I'm continuing to learn each day the truth that absence does indeed make the heart grow fonder.

September 3, 2011

I would rather Speak Five Words with my Mind . . .

One thing that I love about my life abroad @ Handong is the depth of spiritual devotion that I find in nearly all my students and faculty colleagues. There are represented here a wide variety of faith traditions within the Church -- the Body of Christ. Such diversity is, without a doubt, a strength of our university community. With diversity, though, comes the potential for an unbalanced, over-emphasis on certain dimensions of spiritual life and experience. I have recently become even more aware of this likelihood, and my heart is burdened by the possible harm that out-of-balanced teaching and practices may cause, especially in the lives of young people whose hearts are seeking after God and desiring to experience his presence and power in authentic ways. This, however, is not the first time such a concern has arisen in my mind. Early on in my walk with other believers, I encountered several brothers and sisters who taught that the only way to "know" that you were blessed and empowered by God to live a life following after Christ was to have a special spiritual experience where you spoke audibly in the hearing of others with ecstatic utterances -- what these teachers called "unknown tongues" -- that is, not an actual human language that one had not previously learned, but rather a series of sounds emanating from your mouth that they claimed were an evidence of God's presence and work through your physical body.

After first encountering this teaching, I asked my spiritual mentor to help me understand whether this was a pathway of spirituality that I should pursue. As a wise mentor and guide, he pointed me to the Scriptures, and in particular to First Corinthians, chapters 12, 13 and 14. He said this was the portion of the New Testament that spoke most directly to the exercise of spiritual gifts, including what the Bible calls the "gift of tongues." He explained that the Apostle Paul was actually answering questions in this passage that had been previously raised by the believers at the church in Corinth. Paul's main point in response, my mentor said, was to remind the Corinthians that all of the gifts of the Spirit of God were given so that followers of Christ might be enabled to build-up and strengthen others. Their purpose is not individual benefit, but rather the benefit of the whole body.

He also stressed that whatever spiritual gift I may think God has given me that gift must always be exercised out of a heart of love for others. He taught me that this is the main point of Chapter 13. Speaking in tongues, whether they be the languages of men or of angels, is worthless unless it is an expression of love to others. He then went on to show me that love is demonstrated when we speak in such a way that others who hear us understand what we are saying. If I speak aloud in the hearing of others in a way that they do not understand, I am not loving them. I am not edifying them. Only when the unknown language is interpreted and others then understand the message is there any potential for their benefit -- their edification. My mentor also taught me that some Christians practice speaking in tongues as a private prayer language when they are alone.

He noted that there was even a mention of this type of private "prayer language" practice in 1 Corinthians 14, verse 2, where Paul describes the one who is "speaking to God and not to men." Such a private practice of tongues, when not in the hearing of others, is consistent with the overall point of the instruction that Paul is giving in this passage, however, it is a practice that focuses the believer's attention inward rather than outward toward others. In contrast to private expressions, in the cases where audible words or sounds are spoken in the hearing of others, my spiritual mentor said, those words and sounds should either be directly understood by the ones hearing them (that is, they should be spoken in a known, common, human language) or they should be interpreted immediately so that all may understand and benefit. (See 1 Corinthians 14:26-33).

The aim of all audible expression among gatherings of believers should be mutual edification and common blessing. In fact, Paul also warns that if this practice is not followed, then unbelievers who might happen to come in to the gathering would be confused and think that those speaking in expressions that are not understandable are out of their minds. (1 Corinthians 14:23). As followers of Christ, we are charged to pursue the well-being of others before our own individual spirituality. "So with yourselves, since you are eager for manifestations of the Spirit, strive to excel in building up the church." (1 Corinthians 12:12)

At the conclusion of this passage, Paul reiterates the importance of doing all things that can be seen and heard by others in ways that will build them up. He evens uses a proportional argument to show how important it is to speak in an understandable manner whenever what we say can be heard by others. Five words that can be understood -- spoken with "my mind" -- are more important than speaking 10,000 words in non-interpreted and unknowable expressions.

The proper balance is struck when we pray and sing with both our spirit and our mind. (1 Corinthians 14:15). If we truly desire to be loving others as Christ loved us, then we should pursue practices that build others up with the clear and understandable proclamation of God's Word. Let us press on to maturity as we seek to live our lives for others, even as Christ so lived for us!

> *Nevertheless, in church I would rather speak five words with my mind in order to instruct others, than ten thousand words in a tongue. Brothers, do not be children in your thinking. Be infants in evil, but in your thinking be mature.* (1 Corinthians 14:19-20)

17

February 12, 2012

"People of Yangon, I perceive that you are very religious."

I've just returned to Handong after spending 16 days in Myanmar -- "the Land of the Golden Pagodas." This photo was taken during my walk through the shines of Shwedagon Pagoda, the largest Buddhist pagoda in the entire world. I felt that I had a greater sense of what Paul experienced when he walked through the shines and temples of Athens (Acts 17:16-34). I was invited to Myanmar to help teach and train pastors, church leaders and missionaries who serve among the ethnic tribes and native Burmese. What I found, though, was a study in contrasts.

Myanmar (formerly known as Burma) was once one of the most well-developed countries in all of Southeast Asia. Now, it is re-emerging from third-world status that has characterized it over the past 50 years. As a result, contrasts between wealth and poverty abound. On one street, you may find a brand-new high-rise building under construction next to a derelict, dilapidated structure. Rather than repair and renovate them, most buildings are left to deteriorate. On one side of the river, a modern city is rising, while on the other side, the people of a primitive village eek out an agrarian existence.

But the greatest contrast of all is a spiritual one. The vast majority of people are cultural Buddhists and over 1.8 million are monks or nuns who daily walk the streets offering prayers in exchange for gifts of rice, fruits and vegetables. There is, though, a substantial minority of Christians who are the spiritual children of such servants of God as Adoniram Judson. While their numbers may be small in contrast to the followers of other faiths, the devotion of believers in Myanmar was a true encouragement and challenge to my heart. Many of these believers gather in small home churches in the villages to worship and hear God's Word. Others meet in well-established churches within Yangon and other cities. Bible colleges and seminaries have been founded throughout the country to form and equip leaders for the churches and workers who take the Gospel to the un-reached Burmese Buddhist in the villages. As I visited among the believers in Myanmar, I realized that the needs of the churches in this country are, in fact, the same needs that exist in churches in all countries, whether developed or emerging.

There is first the need for servant leaders among the churches. The church in Burma, as well as in Korea and America, already has its fill of men and women who seek to dominate and compel the obedience of others not by their Christ-like example, but by an appeal to institutional position and title. What is truly needed, though, are followers of Christ who seek to serve others according to the pattern of Christ's life -- by bearing the burdens of others. Second, there is the desperate need for the teaching of God's Word. All too often, ministries are started and churches are operated according to human ideas and worldly practices. There is a sad lack of Biblical teaching beyond the fundamental truths of the Gospel. When church policy decisions must be made, most appeal to the intuition of men rather than to the principles of Scripture. And once decisions are made, there is a lack of willingness to subject those decisions to the scrutiny of Scripture. These two needs, though, are no more prominent in the churches of Myanmar than they are in the churches of America.

In contrast to what I've found in American churches, however, Myanmar has in abundance among its believers those who desire and are willing to follow their Lord wherever He leads without attachment to this present world. And it is the evidence of that desire in the words and actions of these dear brothers and sisters that compels my heart to remain open to future calls for further service to the people of this beautiful land.

Februrary 29, 2012

Some might say . . . ."Well, its about time!!"

Here I am at the beginning of my fifth semester of teaching at Handong. When I first was thinking about teaching abroad, (more than three years ago) colleagues who had done so strongly urged me to make the most of my experience by learning the language of my host country. But, I've never been very good at learning, and even worse at speaking, modern languages. Give me Koine Greek or Classical Latin -- you know, those dead languages that no one speaks any more!! "Semper ubi sub ubi!!" I still remember that maxim from my high school Latin teacher at St. Paul's in Concordia.

So . . . I've resisted the counsel of my colleagues and the advice of my loving spouse, who, by the way, started her language lessons within two weeks of arrival here in the Spring of 2010. Within one semester, she had already excelled far beyond my "An yong ha se yo" and "Gam sa ham ni da!" -- which have been my main stays for the past two years! I've resisted that is, until now. This evening, I experienced my first lesson in Korean! And while I've been told that Korean is one of the most difficult languages to learn, and even with my built-in, hard-wired, left brain-right brain-disability with language-learning (primarily, I would contend, because I'm a visual rather than an auditory learner) I found my lesson this evening to be exceptionally fascinating as well as intellectually stimulating.

Korean is a very "scientific language" -- that is, the formation of both the consonant and vowel sounds follow a very rational, logical progression. My tutor, Ms. Damiya Park, demonstrated how the vowel sounds progress from those made with the mouth wide open to those made with it increasingly closed. As I saw the sounds being produced and heard them expressed, they began to make sense even to this lingua-dumbie!

Now, I must confess that I find other Asian languages, such as Chinese and the Chin language of Myanmar, to be much more melodious. But, the precision of Korean is beginning to rival what I had previously believed to be only the province of the ancient classical tongues. There was, however, one very disappointing discovery. I say disappointing, but it was also a very enlightening insight into how language shapes our view of the world. I asked my tutor to tell me the Korean word for "dove." The word is 비둘기 (pronounced "bi dool gi"). It means "pigeon." There is no separate word in Korean for "dove." So if I were to quote the Song of Solomon to my beautiful wife telling her that she had "dove's eyes" (see Song of Songs 1:15), I would say in Korean, "You have pigeon's eyes." Not as romantic as Solomon's words to the Shulamite.

So, in this case, it might not work for me to advise my young male Korean students to master the poetry of Solomon as they make their preparations to woo the woman of their dreams. Well, so much for Korean as a language of love; at least that is, in translation. I hear, though, that I still have much to learn both about and from the Korean language, which admonition I readily accept and yield to. So . . . . off to start my homework! It is indeed about time that I started!

March 20, 2012

Though He Fall, He Will Not Be Utterly Cast Down . . . . .

I have done my fair share of stupid things, but this past Friday afternoon will have to go down in the annuls of my life experiences as one of my stupidest. Here's the picture of the "unbalanced man." I was hurrying across campus heading back to my apartment. In one hand, I was carrying an over-weight bag of groceries and in the other, my mobile phone. My first mistake: hurrying. My second: carrying too many groceries in just one bag rather than separating them out into two. My third: attempting to retrieve a text message while walking too fast and carrying too many groceries in one bag. These three added together caused me to be distracted from the path I was upon and consequently, to completely lose my balance when I stepped-up upon a large rock that leads up a small hill along a short-cut to the faculty apartments.

In this unbalanced state, I fell back and to my left landing with a resounding thump upon the cold, hard Handong ground. The mid-section of my left rib cage absorbed the brunt of the impact and pain immediately followed. How more stupid could I have been? That was the persistent question that pressed hard upon my dizzying thoughts as I laid there catching the breath that had been knocked out of me. In time, I rolled over and sat up, still a bit light-headed, though. Eventually, I regained my footing, gathering up the groceries that had been strewn about by the fall, and resumed my journey, now walking much more slowly and deliberately along the sidewalk and up the road to my apartment. I was able to prepare the lunch that I had been rushing to complete, but with a new found awareness of the realities of life -- a new thorn in my flesh for which I now need Christ's sustaining grace all the more to bear.

After heeding the wise advice of a caring colleague, I went later in the afternoon to the hospital and found from the doctor's exam and x-ray's that the fall had caused nearly inch-long cracks in two of my left ribs. Now, four days on, the pain in my side persists reminding me night and day of my on-going need to slow down and give thanks for the goodness of our God.

That goodness has been lavished upon this poor miserable, stupid, unbalanced man by the gracious, tender kindnesses of his students, family and friends who have been attending to his care with many visits, thoughtful prayers, meal preparations, dish-washings, house-cleanings, telephone calls, and the sweetest text and Facebook messages throughout his days and pain-filled nights. Through these and in so many other ways, I have been overcome by the love of our God who promises that, though I fall, and surely I do every day, I will not be utterly cast down, because the Lord upholds me by His hand. Psalm 37:24

Reflection

18

You don't need a Map, When you have a Guide

During my years of teaching at Handong, I would often recount for my students life lessons I learned from experiences with my children. One story that I told nearly every semester conveys one of the most important of those lessons. It happened one summer's weekend along the Ozark Trail in Southern Missouri when my sons Caleb and Justin and I were on a hike. We had followed the trail markers for several miles and came upon a tree that was marked in an unusual manner. Upon our closer inspection, we learned that this particular tree had been designated by the original trail surveyor as a "witness tree."

A witness tree is landmark that a surveyor will name in the legal description of the property survey as "witnessing" or "testifying" to a particular point, usually a corner point, within the surveyed property. For us, the witness tree marked the trail we were seeking to follow. Bright yellow diamond-shaped emblems had been fixed to north, south, east and west sides of the tree's trunk, so that the tree's special significance could readily be seen from every direction. The first surveyor had so marked this witness tree to serve as a guide for those who would come along the trail after him. Having observed the tree, we passed along and made our way to a campsite for the night. The following day, we set out again upon the trail but soon ventured off the marked path to follow what appeared to be an old logging road. It meandered through the woods for several miles and then came to an abrupt dead-end in the thick of the forest. Where were we to go? We could back-track along the path we had hiked to the point where we first departed the marked trail, or we could blaze our way through the woods. We had no map. But, as we were about to learn, you don't need a map when you have a guide. In this case, though, our guide was not a person who was present with us, but one who had gone before us and marked the way. As we looked carefully through the undergrowth, Caleb spotted in the distance a bright yellow diamond – one of the markers we had observed the day before on the witness tree. We set our sights on the witness tree and made our way through the thicket until we reached our destination. Our guide had returned us to the trail we were meant to follow.

And so it is in life, we may venture off the path, but when we seek to follow the way that is meant for us, our guide will show us the way. We may rarely know in advance where that path may take us, but we can always be confident that One has gone before who will guide us. My path led me to respond to a call to come and teach in Korea. I continued to follow that guidance for another two years until the path once again led me to return to Missouri, this time, though, not to teaching at a university, but to service as a pastor to a local congregation of a Korean-American church. But that's another story for another day.

Made in the USA
Lexington, KY
23 January 2018